Can You Squeeze My Banana?

Brenda Wojick

AuthorHouse™
1663 Liberty Drive
Bloomington, IN 47403
www.authorhouse.com
Phone: 1-800-839-8640

© 2010 Brenda Wojick. All rights reserved.

No part of this book may be reproduced, stored in a retrieval system, or
transmitted by any means without the written permission of the author.

First published by AuthorHouse   8/26/2010

ISBN: 978-1-4520-5852-8 (e)
ISBN: 978-1-4520-5850-4 (sc)
ISBN: 978-1-4520-5851-1 (hc)

Library of Congress Control Number: 2010911186

Printed in the United States of America
Bloomington, Indiana

This book is printed on acid-free paper.

Because of these people my book is here!!!

First, to my parents, Bill and Paula Forster, thank you for planning my arrival back in 1970. If it weren't for your love and support spread out over 40 years I would have never accomplished this project. You both taught me I can do anything I wanted, so I did. I love you both more than you can imagine.

To my husband, Fred Scott Wojick, for dealing with me every step of the way and loving me every minute of it. I love you back even more! We make one perfect couple!

To all of my awesome kids, Alyssa, Tayla, Marc Ginnetti and Gabriella Wojick,I love you all very much! Thanks for living in my crazy world, although you didn't really have a choice… LOL.

To Karen Wieber, my amazing friend who has provided me with the courage each and every day to be the best nurse I can be, but to also follow my dream and write this book, and to Lois Lavoie you laughed every step of the way as I told you these stories and added them to my book. I needed that. I love ya, and thanks to you both!

….and Joann Lynds my friend of 40 years

Acknowledgements

To Kelly Burke who actually brought this hilarious comment to my attention, therefore providing me with a great title for my book.

To Jill Messender for proof reading my book night after night just to get it right.

Dana Andrews for all of his awesome artwork.

Definition and Nature of the Work

Registered nurses (RNs) work to promote good health and prevent illness. They educate patients and the public about various medical conditions; treat patients and help in their rehabilitation; and provide advice and emotional support to patients' families. RNs use considerable judgment in providing a wide variety of services.

Many registered nurses are general-duty nurses who focus on the overall care of patients. They administer medications under the supervision of doctors and keep records of symptoms and progress. General-duty nurses also supervise licensed practical nurses (LPNs), nursing aides, and orderlies.

RNs can specialize: (1) by work setting or type of treatment—critical-care nurses work in intensive care units, and psychiatric nurses treat patients with mental health disorders; (2) by disease, ailment, or condition—HIV/AIDS nurses care for patients with HIV infection and AIDS, and

Brenda Wojick

addictions nurses treat patients with substance abuse problems; (3) by organ or body system—nephrology nurses care for patients with kidney disease, and respiratory nurses treat patients with disorders such as asthma; and (4) by population—school nurses provide care for children and adolescents in school, while geriatric nurses provide care for the elderly. RNs may also work in combined specialties, such as pediatric oncology (the care of children and adolescents with cancer) or cardiac emergency (the care of patients with heart problems in emergency rooms).

Some RNs choose to become advanced-practice nurses and get special training beyond their RN education. They are often considered primary health care practitioners and work independently or in collaboration with physicians. (1)

WAITRESS

The job description for a waitress would be to seat the guests, take the drink orders, and watch to see if the guests need anything. Body language lets you know when they are ready to order. When they are ready you take the order, make sure they are served drinks, appetizers. Clean tables, Fill salt, things like that. Make silverware rolls, if they use those in the establishment. Keep checking on guests, make sure they are happy. Fix whatever drinks, keep the tables going. Help the busboys. Things get really busy for wait staff. It can also depend on the establishment too. You basically keep the guests happy.

Where I work we don't have busboys, so we do everything, clear tables, wash dishes... everything.

Servant - one that serves others <a public *servant*> ; *especially* : one that performs duties about the person or home of a master or personal employer(3)

Remember these comparisons, you will see the similarities.

It's Just For Fun

Everything that is written here is all in good fun. It does not and never will undermine the fact that myself and millions of nurses lack empathy or compassion. This will enlighten you as a non-healthcare professional as to a day in the life of a registered nurse. It demonstrates how we have bad days just like the next person. It is difficult to always be nice, but we do so with professionalism and respect. Some days the compassion cup is completely full because with some of the people our patience wears very thin, but we still continue to work with our patients and treat them with the dignity that they deserve. Every comedian needs a story and I've found mine and it happens to be my work as a nurse.

I have been a registered nurse for five years. Many of the girls that I work with who are close to my age already have 10 plus years under their belt. In my brief number of years I have learned more than I ever needed to know, and have seen far too much, in fact, probably more than I would have ever liked to see. In a world of text messages, computers and cell phones, you must have heard the slang phrase TMI (too much information) well, that is what my everyday life on the job

Can You Squeeze My Banana?

has become - TMI. It's just too much! The truth of the matter is this is my job, and I would not trade it for the world, but some days I would like to tweak it a little smidge.

There are many things I realized very early on in my career. There is absolutely, positively no room for a nurse to have a weak stomach, wobbly knees and an overactive sense of smell! If you do nursing just isn't for you!

You see, in the real world of nursing at a very real hospital, not at the City of Hope Hospital from *Grey's Anatomy*, the floor will most likely smell like a big ole' farm from the Midwest. In every breath you take we inhale odors that you never thought were even possible to ingest. It will take your breath away and singe every damn nose hair. The aroma of any farm would be an improvement from the poop smell that I walk into every day. Occasionally, more times than not, some patients may actually poop right there in front of you. I've learned from the very beginning to just deal with it because every other nurse on your floor is floating on the same shit log that you've set sail on. The race begins at 7am and for some of us it ends at 3:30 when we clock out. If you make it across the finish line on time, you are definitely a hero because in the nurse's handbook, YOU NEVER GET OUT ON TIME. 3:30 is just an approximation.

More food for thought: Nursing is a never ending learning experience. You will never see the same situation twice, and if you thought you

Brenda Wojick

would never see the same person twice, think again because people love to rack up their frequent flyer miles, and they just keep coming back. I do not think that they realize the more miles they get there is really no bonus flight at the end. You may occasionally earn a trip to the CCU (critical care unit) depending on the severity of your condition, so other than that just stay home.

I work on a medical surgical respiratory floor, and to put it in layman's terms, I see anyone from the age of 18 and up to even 102. At 102 I would really like to be worm food at that time, but who am I to say. I get to divulge into the lives of many, get up close and personal, and I get to ask the questions that no one wants to ask and no one ever feels comfortable answering. For instance, do you drink? How much? Then I double what they say because absolutely no one admits to their true consumption of alcohol. I probably wouldn't either. I then get a bucket of popcorn, pull up a seat in the front row, and watch them detox. These patients are always a very special treat to take care of as they spit on you when they talk, pee on you when they're standing, and they expel putrid odor when they talk to you. When dealing with a person who is detoxing, remember to buy two cups of coffee and drive really slow to work that day

Have you ever been in an abusive relationship? The patient isn't going to give you a truthful answer because their loved one will beat the ever lovin' shit out of them if they find out that they have confided

Can You Squeeze My Banana?

in me. Dah! Either that or the person is 86 and their spouse has died already and now I've touched upon a sensitive spot in their life because they miss their life partner of 60 something years. Do you smoke? By far this is my favorite question. The floor that I work on day in and day out specializes in respiratory care, so this is always an interesting question and much more so because 9 out of 10 times when I ask the question, the patient has expiratory wheezes that are incredibly loud it sounds like air being let out of a balloon, and I can hear this from the elevator in the hallway. I'll just put the stethoscope down because I can pretty much say they are a wheezy smoking chimney. He or she won't have to prove it either because I can tell by the yellow fingernails and the stale smell on their clothes. It is when they tell you that they don't smoke that truly amuse me because they reek of smoke and I've found a lighter on them and a pack of cigarettes hiding in their sheets. Oh, by now they are yelling at me because they are having a nicotine fit, and I can smell actual smoke coming from their bathroom because the windows at our hospital do not open because of the underlying fear that a patient may jump out the window, and you know what? I wouldn't put anything past a person who is having a nicotine fit.

I love to ask a person, "how is your diet?" Nine times out of ten the person is unhealthy and overweight. The large lady or gentleman looks at me as if to say, "how does my diet look to you, you idiot?"

Brenda Wojick

But by far the best question ever is, "When was your last bowel movement?" To many this seems like an odd question, but for me it's just so exciting to see what the patient's response is going to be. People often ask me, "Why the hell do you need to know that?" The truth is I personally really don't care, but this is my job. The elderly really love to talk about their bowel movements. The world comes to an end if they do not have a bowel movement each and every day at the same time, the same place and if it doesn't look exactly the same way it did the day before. You ask any elderly person, and they can talk to you endlessly about their shit.

Here are some common questions in nursing to ponder, and the answers that I am truly waiting for.

Q. "Did you move your bowels today?"

A. " Yeah."

Q. " Large or small?"

A. " God damn huge."

Q. "What did it look like?"

A. "The Loch Ness monster."

Q. "So, are you saying it was big and curly?"

A. " I'm sayin' it was huge."

Q. " Could you smell it?"

A. " Smelled like shit."

Q. " Did you poke it?"

A. " Felt like shit."

Q."Sir, did it appear to be shit that you did this morning?"

A." Yep."

That would be by far the best conversation ever, and I've had similar dialogue with patients. My point in highlighting the exchange above is that some people do offer a lot more information than what you are asking them for, but then again I am asking them a truly personal question.

Everyone poops, everyone pees, people are their own individual and yet the same as the next person…quite ironic. We all sneeze, we fart, we will all have a drippy nose at one time or another, but some will choose to leave it, and I prefer to wipe it. He smells, she doesn't, but she only has one tooth and she spits when she speaks. This could be your mother, your brother or your baby's daddy. I get to take care of you while you are here confined to your hospital room for hopefully a brief period of time. I'll go in your room, breath through my mouth, catch a whiff and attempt to change the subject while backing out of the room. Like it or not, at some point we all may get sick and end up at some hospital. No one is the only one, there will always be someone before you and someone after you, there is a revolving door policy. The truth is that he or she may really be sick or just need a vacation. I see it all. The nurses, doctors, nurses aides, dietary department.….the list goes on, but we have the extreme pleasure of taking care of you. The patients are alert and oriented or horribly confused. Either way I look at them and pray that someday that will not be me. I prefer being on the outside looking in, but at least I know what I'm in for should I ever find myself on the other side of the bed. You should read this collection knowing that I see life optimistically, but I can't help it if the occasional cynical thought sneaks in. So laugh out loud. After all, laughter is the best medicine!

It only takes me 15 minutes to drive from my house (not including the stop to get my large cup of java, decaf, one sweet and low, mocha swirl) to get up the highway to get to work. At 6:20 am there are a limited number of cars on the road. It's not until I am actually on the highway that I finally begin to see color mingling with the dark of night. It's going to be another beautiful day that I won't get to see today because I will be spending 8 of my hours confined behind the dreary brick walls of the hospital. I am no different than any other working female who will not see the summer sun today.

It's too god damn early for me. My eyes are like tiny little slits right now. I can't open them. I am definitely not a morning person, but I make a valiant attempt as I multitask in the car, blaring radio keeping me awake, window half way down, no matter what the temperature is outside. I'm fumbling with my coffee cup so that I can keep my eyes on the road and I dribble it on my nicely creased scrub pants. I then forget that I have mascara on my eyes and I just rubbed them.. I guess it's better than drool on my mouth. As I try to fix the mess in my mirror, I

Can You Squeeze My Banana?

grab my cell phone to call my kids and wake them up. Looking in the mirror I see a piece of granola bar stuck in the middle of my two front teeth. Now that's attractive but I suppose it's better I see it while in the car than while I'm leaning over a patient checking for their pulse. After I pick it out I am finally ready to start my day.

I arrive in the parking lot across the street from the hospital at 6:42 am. I don't know how this happens, but I get there the same darn time every day. There it is, standing tall across the street, "THE HOSPITAL." For some people hospitals are intimidating, for me it's just work. This building may not be as overwhelming as a large Boston city hospital that casts a shadow on the Boston skyline, but it is a pretty serious place if you work there every day.

The front of the building is brand spankin' new. All new construction, very appealing to one's eye, welcoming patients and visitors, an architectural monument to excellent medical care, however I don't really get to see the front of the building very often because I, as well as all other hospital employees, enter the building from the employee entrance. I'm making my way over to the green cross walk to get to the other side, and cars are just flying by me…Where the hell are they going in such a rush? They are going into the same parking lot that I just came from. Whatever happened to pedestrians having the right of way?

I am scurrying across the street and my ugly work bag is bobbling against my hip bone, causing my underwear to favor the right butt cheek only. I can't pick it now because I am afraid someone will be walking behind me. If I don't pick it, and I just leave it, it becomes a wedgie. Its tough to start my day with lop sided undies. Now I am almost running because I really want to wiggle out of the wedgie and specks of coffee are burning my nose hairs as I drink and run at the time. Don't try this at home.

I make my way up to the third floor. I can't breathe as I jog my way up the stairs from the second to the third floor. When did I get so old?

I thought the toughest part of my morning was the alarm clock going off and waking me up. Nope. The hardest part of my day begins behind the closed doors leading onto the floor. I push them open, and I get to save lives. NAH! Sounds good though, but I really don't do this at all. On some occasions I get to prolong someone's life whether they want me to or not. For the most part I am maintaining one. If you don't have those three little but very powerful consonants written on a piece of paper (DNR) with your name next to it, then I make sure you remain on earth at least one more day, so like it or not, you are here to stay. I won't lie, being an RN is intriguing, and I get a great sense of satisfaction from my job or I would not be working in the healthcare field.

In The Beginning

"Never pick a fight with an ugly person, they've got nothing to loose"

Robin Williams

She was an average size female, 5 feet 3 inches tall, weighing approximately 150 lbs., blonde hair and piercing blue eyes that just jabbed you when you got even slightly close to her. She lived with a

Brenda Wojick

constant scowl on her face. I don't understand how one person could always look so miserable, but she was a fine example. In the classroom she was seated in the far corner casting a very stern, controlling look from her face, and then the introduction…I am Sister Ann. She's a nun! Not oh shit, bullshit, cut-the-shit, but what we have here is holy shit! I didn't even know they fabricated nuns anymore! I assumed they were out of style just like the 80's, but then just like the 80's, those days are coming back, and apparently nuns are too. Ironically, I am praying to god at that moment, "Please God, don't let this be happening to me." It was then I was punished for asking god not to let me learn from one of his saviors, and that's when I realized I was going to live in purgatory for seven long weeks. Believe me, it was a long road to hell and back.

Anyway, Sister would very quickly acquire a certain nickname from me, and I would be very gracious and pass it onto my entire clinical group so that they too knew just what name to call her by. This nickname suited her personality to a perfect ball and socket fit. So in my best efforts to protect her identity I will enlist her nickname in this book, Sister Satan. Her name continues to send chills down my spine each and every time I mutter it. I will never forget her because she was my absolute worst nightmare ever, but luckily I was not alone in this misery. I had six other girls that were going to share in my misfortune, and they would have to deal with Sister Satan herself. While the rest of the students were enjoying their first semester of nursing school, I was attending boot camp with the drill sergeant herself. Relentless would be a mild adjective for the wild untamed beast and her despicable behavior towards me and us. Now, I will take you on my never ending 7 week painful journey that is etched in my mind forever.

One word could sum up my entire semester of school, retarded. It seems cruel to say, but it fits mighty fine. When you are a student in nursing school you give up your life that you once knew is now no longer. No family time, no movies, no friends, it's all over. The rules of the game before me were simple. Every day of each month, you are being evaluated on your clinical performance and then "passed off," so to say, on certain tasks that we must perform hands on and confidently in front of the instructor. Being passed off means you get to have the instructors little tiny teeny weenie initials next to your name after that particular task. Her initials should have been BS. It doesn't seem like much, but this demonstrates to her that we are competent individuals and safe enough to perform clinical duties on our own. Well, big blue eyes, and I am not referring to Frank Sinatra, decided that she would not pass me off on the task of simple basic hand washing. Hand washing people!! For some reason I do not consider this a big clinical event. I know the importance of hand washing, but her instruction is to the extreme. We are talking about an everyday event. While every other clinical group was beyond this sophisticated ordeal, our group was being lectured and pulled through the mud day after day as if this were a continuous

Brenda Wojick

tragic event. Nobody died here sister girl, perhaps a fingernail went unnoticed, but still no tragedy. I would like to go back a bit and state, "this is pure bullshit."

Each day one by one we were "summonsed" into the bathroom at a local hospital where we were doing our clinical rotation and the rest of us waited right outside the bathroom door. The door remained open, thank you lord up above, so we could at least see the faces of our other peers; otherwise I would have had the biggest anxiety attack ever, and probably would have hyperventilated my way to the emergency room. I must say that the hand washing performance resembled an exorcism. Was this woman really serious? She couldn't be. I felt like there were hidden cameras somewhere. Am I on "Bloopers and Blunders?" I'm being Punked right? Ashton Kutcher is popping out any minute. Hell no. This is real. Blue eyed Satan was more serious than God himself!

It was my turn! With buckling knees, sweat on my brown, and vomit making its way up my throat, she pointed to me as if I were in serious trouble, and with my head hung low I stepped up to the sink. It was a little tiny porcelain white sink like all hospitals have. I may have actually thrown up a little bit in my mouth, and I was holding that fart in that really, really needed to come out because I was so nervous. Boy that gas bubble was turning my stomach. It pains me to reminisce about this day. It is sort of like post traumatic stress disorder. Here it goes…I turned the water on, apply the soap, and I began to wash my

Can You Squeeze My Banana?

hands in a proper nursing fashion which is washing from the elbows down thinking to myself, "How could I go wrong, it's friggin' hand washing." She, in the nastiest voice ever, was barking at me, and for the first five minutes I didn't know what she was saying. Then I listened closely, "You are not doing it right, more friction, friction. Rub harder. Rub faster. Friction, friction!!!" I had never yelled that loud even when I was giving birth to my three children. At this point I felt like I was ripping the skin off of my hands, and I felt like I was the star in a porn movie gone bad with her yelling at me "FRICTION." MTV could have a field day with this one, "GOOD NURSES GONE WILD," and next would be "NAUGHTY NURSING INSTRUCTORS. FRICTION, FAST AND FURIOUS. It could be a whole series. She was so frustrated with my "performance" that she was not going to pass me off of this particular clinical unless I learned that more friction was needed in hand washing, and apparently lots and lots of it. Bloody knuckles and callous palms meant nothing to this woman. But what was totally apparent to me and my new friends was that Sister Satan had been a nun for way to long and Sister really needed to get some friction herself. I was not sure which team she played for men or women, whichever! It didn't matter at this point. She was horrible, terrifying even. Was I in trouble, oh yes, this was going to be the semester from hell!

Each and every day with this lady brought about a new nightmare. As Sister Satan told us, she was a nurse in the military, as if being a nun wasn't bad enough she was a militant nun and boy was she ever so serious about making a bed. Not only had I been washing my hands for 33 years, but I had also been making my bed for about 25 of those 33 years. Now I'd just discovered, thank god for Sister, that I had been doing it all wrong, and I could have seriously been injured while making a bed. Are you f***ing kidding me. Who the hell would have known this crap that she is about to bore me with. I was shocked, and stunned indeed when she proceeded to teach. Nip this, tuck that, pull that up, and push it down. $30,000 and three student loans later that I will die paying, low and behold, I can make the perfect bed. Oh, hell yeah! Now that must go on my resume because I am so sure that all of the hospitals around Boston are probably looking for that. But, anyway, in the making of the perfect bed, I discovered that the seam of a pillow case must face up towards the wall and not down towards the foot of the bed where the patient's neck will lie. I bet you're wondering why and what the hell am I talking about? I will share with you that according to Sister the seam may hurt the patient's neck. What seam on any pillow case have you ever known to injure a person? Even in my nursing career today, no patient has ever been admitted to the hospital's emergency room for a "seam injury" to their neck. Can you image hearing, "let's get that patient into Cat Scan right away. She fell into her bed and hit her head on the seam of her pillow case." I didn't even realize that there was a damn seam on any of my pillow cases for that matter, and I've

Can You Squeeze My Banana?

slept on them for many years let alone pull a neck muscle on one of them. I know this will shock you, but I made the bed wrong because the "seam" was not facing up as I was told. Yep, it was facing down. I could have seriously hurt a patient she told me. I felt awful indeed! Nah, just kidding. I didn't give it a second thought.

I woke up the next day and went to the hospital for my rotation. I met up with my classmates, and I was holding my neck as if it were stiff. I was sort of massaging it, moaning a little bit, and of course they asked what I did. Well, I slept on my pillow the wrong way, can you believe it. The damn seam was the wrong way and look at what happened. I have a crick in my neck. I so badly wanted to wear a neck brace so that Sister would ask why, but I had a funny little feeling that she wouldn't appreciate a good sense of humor. She didn't appreciate anything for that matter

Being a mature adult, only part of the time, I enjoy my personal space, and Sister Satan did not recognize this at all. Mandated personal space for me was 18 inches all the way around my body. This lady grabbed the top of my arm one too many times. As I would go to clinical each time I carried around a pen in my hand, a pen that clicked on the top. I was always misplacing pens, and you need a black pen at all times, and I also believe it was a nervous habit that I had. So what! If Bob Dole can do the pen thing so can I. This woman was supposed to be a compassionate, caring follower of god. Tah! She would rip the pen out of my hand day after day after day and put it in my pocket as if it was bothering her. It felt as if I was a child and she was punishing me. Ahhh, memories of my Old Catholic school days. I can almost hear the song playing in the background. Whatever! She never learned because tomorrow's another day, and I was going to have another pen that clicked at the top and do the same thing partially out of nervousness and partially because I just wanted to piss her off at this point. She had it out for my black clicky pen, and oh yeah, me too! (Remember this story, it will come back)

My days go on and like the old cliché, same old stuff different day, hand washing and bed making until the moment Sister tells me that my hair isn't back tight enough. Is she for real is what I'm thinking. It is up in a bun (old school) off my collar and my face is so distorted, so tightly pulled back I look almost Asian. I also want to mention the use of a bottle of gel and a can of hairspray. Can I get some kind of reimbursement for this please? I can barely see what the heck I am doing because my eyes are so skewed. Joan Rivers, eat your heart out.

Do you ever get flyaway hair? One little piece that just gets into your face, you have no idea how it ever came out of the hairspray net in the first place, but it did. You can barely see it with the naked eye it's so microscopic. Well, I had one of those little hairs that day apparently. I never realized it, but Sister Satan did because she called me over and ripped the damn thing right out of the side of my head. I was like; oh no you didn't just rip my hair out of my head. I was in shock! I had no clue what to say and then I'm thinking I should retaliate by hitting her in the head with a pillow seam or something, but I will be sure to flunk out of this very long agonizing semester. I wanted to bitch slap this lady, or quite possibly pull a Mike Tyson and bite her friggin ear off. All I could say was, "Did you just rip a piece of hair out of my head?" She acted like this was nothing. I wanted to retaliate and rip a piece of hair out of her head. This lady's only license should be that of a Registered Certified Nut job! She needs a round white padded room.

Clinical review day came for me, the end of the rotation, and Sister Satan must provide us with our reviews on how we did in her clinical underworld. Hah! I walked into the hallway of our school prepared for whatever she was going to declare to me, but I had one little last joke for Sister. You see, my oldest daughter had won this pen in her class for selling candy or something like that, and the pen was about 12 inches long and 1-2 inches in diameter with the biggest push button on the top that you could ever imagine, and it made the best clicking noise ever. Bull's eye! I clipped it to the top of the collar on my shirt, and it came down to oh, right below my boob. In my own subtle way, this is going to be how I say "bite me" without getting into trouble. It's not mean, it's not cruel, but it will certainly get my point across. It is what it is people. My friends could not believe I was going to do this, in fact they dared me, and I had no problem taking the dare. It wasn't so bad; I think it's

Brenda Wojick

better than hitting her with a pillow. I wouldn't want her to get hurt by the seam, if you know what I mean. I clipped it to my shirt, and away I went. I walked into the classroom ever so proudly, pen attached to me and a sweet little grin on my face. I sat down ever so seriously and listened to what she had to say to me. All constructive criticism which usually I can take had it come from someone else's mouth. In the end, I had to sign a paper stating I agree with her ridiculous comments. "Sign here, Brenda," Sister stated to me. "Sure." Remember the bionic man how he did everything in slow motion to show his strength, well this is exactly what I felt like as I took the pen off of my collar, clicked the huge button at the top to show the pen's tip, and began to sign the paper with this pen. It was so awkward and difficult to hold I felt slightly retarded, but I chuckled as I did it as the pen swayed side to side. I can imagine how ridiculous this looked, and she sat there stone faced staring at me. Man, if looks could kill I would have fallen on the floor. "Like my pen, Sister?" I snidely said to her. "I don't find your sense of humor funny at all," she replied. "I do," as I got up, handed her my review and proceeded to walk out the door. "Have a nice day Sister." I felt awesome. As little as it sounds, I got the last word in, childish yes, gratifying totally!

I might add just for the record, she was so controlling and unprofessional that she only lasted at our school for another 7 week clinical rotation, and then she was let go!

Minor Detail

"If you love your job, you haven't worked a day in your life"
Tommy Lasorda

I was finally out of morning report which took 30 minutes to go through everybody on the even side of the hallway from room four down to twenty, and it appeared that things hadn't changed in the last 24 hours. It was still going to be a hectic day as usual on the 3rd floor. The floor that I work on has the capacity to house 30 patients at a time, and that's packing the patients in. If our census kept up this way, we would be purchasing bunk beds for everyone. Nothing that I hear in report is shocking to me anymore. Actually, today it is quite the opposite because if it looked like it could be a decent day that would make me nervous by every sense of the definition. I grabbed my coffee and my yogurt and made my way down the hallway that just reeks of bad body odor, but it's not body odor, it is the smell of poop 100% pure. It is by far the worst stench that you would ever want to inhale at 7:30 in the morning. It just doesn't get any better than this.

I had my patient assignment fixed to my little black clip board, and I scurried to the nurse's station. It's nothing glamorous by any means. The walls are a dull white as well as the floor, although the floors are buffed pretty darn well. The nurse's station is partly enclosed by glass which at times I wished was camouflaged. The glass still does not stop the unwanted guests from coming into our little working circle, and god forbid a family member or friend should cross the line and step into the area we sit enclosed by the streaked glass it's like they committed the worst offense ever. Some of us have even been known to gasp, "what are they doing in here? Don't they know this is our area?" It is like crossing a picket line, it should never be done. We have a handful of computers that work only part of the time, a rack of charts and some areas where we take the charts from. We have a handful of phones that even at this time in the morning are ringing off the hook. Night shift and morning shift were chatting it up, making sure we see eye to eye about the patients we have adopted for the day. Another thing that I do and most every other nurse does is check the schedule and take a good look around and see who is working with you for the day. This will dictate if your day with suck or not. The crew who are on with you can make you or break you to tiny pieces in an eight hour shift. The stench in the air also dictates if it is going to be a good day or as I said before, a sucky day. It was still early in the morning, so I was trying to be optimistic, and that lasted approximately 5 whole minutes before my post traumatic stress kicks in from the previous day. I said to myself, "take a deep breath self, it's going to be alright."

First things first, I checked in with each of my patients, as I do every day, making sure that they are all alive and well and breathing. By doing this, I can also weed out the problem people and know just who is going to put up a fight today. It was going smoothly so far which had me wondering why. After I came out of room 14 I went to visit the gentleman in room 16. He was in the bed that is closest to the door, so he was the first person I saw when I entered the room. He was rather a fruitless man who appeared extremely glum and gloomy. He was pale white, resembling the color of glue. His eyes were astonishingly droopy as if they were dripping right down off of his face. He was paralyzed not from the stroke that he'd had, but from a lone facial nerve that was severed many years ago which resulted in complete right side facial paralysis. I introduced myself to him as I do to all of my patients. "Good morning, my name is Brenda, and I am going to be your nurse for the day." He began to speak to me with a thick slur due to the facial paralysis. He was very difficult to understand and he was obviously frustrated by this.

Backing the bus up just a tad, beep, beep, beep, in report this morning, I heard from the previous nurse on the night shift that this gentleman was a little hard of hearing. I am a loud person anyway so I figured my piercing voice should suffice, but in this case it doesn't. I

Brenda Wojick

hate to wake anybody else up at this time in the morning though, and he had a roommate to the right of him, but I thought I would have to give it a try.

"How are you feeling today," I said to him after I introduced myself as his nurse for the day. I didn't receive a response, just a blank stare. "Are you having any pain today that I should know about, sir?" Again he looked at me quite despondent as if to say, *a little louder please.* So, being the good little do-be that I am I began to yell much louder to this little guy. "I need to know how you are feeling this morning, and if you are having any pain right now." Those are the selected few questions that could give you a whole lot of answers right away. I was now leaning in much, much closer to him and his face. Any closer and I would be licking the guy. By now he could probably tell that I'd had my morning cup of Joe, but in hopes that he will hear something, anything, I continue to yell. Hello! Anybody home! Everybody on the floor heard me, but he didn't. Then he turned his head towards me, which I thought might be his good ear, and I nearly fell back.

No ear! He has no ear! None, nada. No ear!

What he did have was black necrotic tissue around a hole, and it is a hole that apparently he could not hear out of. The ear that he did have on the other side is no good! Not working! He could just barely hear from it. I felt as if I am staring down into the abyss. How could I

30

excuse myself out of this one? He probably knew damn well that I was freaked out. I hadn't seen anything quite like this before.

Very politely, I left the room, and went out to the nurse's station to share my story. "In report this morning, I found out that my patient is a little hard of hearing, but I go into my patient's room, and he is just looking at me with a blank stare. There is a sign above his bed stating that he is hard of hearing, so with all my energy, and believe me I have a lack of energy this time in the morning I am yelling to him" Now Karen and a few other nurses were behind me listening as they always do with a little smirk on their faces wondering what the heck the punch line to this story was going to be. "Guys, he turns to me and I think he is turning his good ear to me to listen, no, that's not the case. He has no ear! No ear!" I threw my hands up in the air and my face to the wind. I chuckled, with no disrespect to the patient and then I slapped my hand on the desk with force. Of course he doesn't have an ear. Should I have expected anything different? It's a hole, I am yelling into a black hole! Slightly hard of hearing did she say? I let out a deep sigh. Note to self: tell next nurse patient has no ear!

I think I had a BM

"Hard work never killed anybody, but why take a chance?"
Edgar Bergen

While I was going to nursing school, I worked as a nursing assistant on a Geriatric Medical Psychiatric floor. In translation this meant sick, old, crazy people. My intention at the time was to get all of the

Can You Squeeze My Banana?

experience that I could to help prepare me for my career. Oh, did this ever! This floor not only taught me where not to work, but what a "CODE BROWN" was, figuratively and imaginatively speaking of course. This is one of the very first stories that I ever spoke about to my family, friends and to my grandmother Mary who is still my biggest fan. You might say unfortunately, but this was also my inspiration to write this book.

Some of the Geri/psyche patients that I took care of were confined to their beds for one reason or another. It was actually quite sad because these people had medical issues as well as psych issues. Many of them had dementia. They barely knew their own name let alone knew where they were. It was a locked unit, and I had to ring a bell to come in. When the door bell rang, 20 patients would line up by the door in hopes of escaping the unit. It was amazing how quickly a person could grab their belongings and scurry to the door.

One night I was working the 11:00 pm to 7:00 am shift thinking that shift would be oh so nice and quiet. It was pure torture because many of these people were sundowners. This is not as lovely and calming as the word may sound. As soon as the sun went down, these individuals began to act crazy, more confused or even highly agitated. They yelled, they screamed, they hit, and even a few of them attempted to strangle anyone who came in contact with them. When you have a Geri/psych patient is confined to his or her bed when they have to

Brenda Wojick

go to the bathroom- , poopies, the big number 2-they are going to go right where they lay. My job was to clean them up and change the bed without passing out. Before I go on, I feel the need to provide you with the definition of a nursing assistant - They can be found in nursing homes, hospitals, adult day health centers, assisted living facilities, even personal homes. Wherever there is a need for personal care, Certified Nursing Assistants are the ones who, for the most part, perform the most basic needs for patients, young and old alike. They work under the supervision of a nurse. Since aides have extensive daily contact with each patient, they are the very key to providing vital information on the patients' conditions to the nurse. (1) In much less intricate terms a nursing assistant is an ass wiper plain and simple. It should be AW instead of CA or NA- ass wiper big time. That sums up the job in two words. This particular night I had a patient at the end of the hall and for seven straight hours he called "nurse" all night. And by that he meant me, the ass wiper. I would have been lucky to be the nurse that getting stuck in the office doing "paperwork" all night. I could detect the rancid stench from this guy from all the way down the hall! The odor flooded the entire psychiatric floor. He didn't even have to tell me what he needed. Call me psychic, but I just knew. I had been changing, flipping, fluffing, and powdering this guy's butt by myself the entire night. I was extremely flustered and flabbergasted by the whole situation. How many times can a person go in one night? I had been up to my elbows

Can You Squeeze My Banana?

in poop the entire time, and not to mention the threatening odor of the task. My eyes were watering and what I wouldn't do to get my hands on some ammonia pads to ram up my nose. I was even petrified to mouth breathe. Who really knows what kind of effect this toxin could have on my lungs for crying out loud? Who the hell would come get me after I passed out and hit the floor? It might take hours for someone to realize that I was down. There were no emergency buttons, only little bells that the patient rang, like the little silver ones that ding when you walk into dry cleaners. The bells everybody ignore.

Finally, the sun was coming back up and this little guy called me for one last time! "Nurse! I think I had a bowel movement!" The key word here was THINK. No one thinks that they just had a bowel movement. You either know that you shit your pants or you didn't. You even have some idea that if you attempted to fart and oops, a little shit may have come out by accident. I walked into that room, and this guy was up to his earlobes in feces. He was just sitting in it, touching it not having a care in the world. "I think I had a bowel movement miss," he said to me. "You think, you THINK you had a bowel movement," I managed to mutter through my quivering lips. I shook my head in complete and utter defeat. I lost this battle. The battle of the shit pile! It was all over him, and the smell was so mortifying that it made his statement completely ridiculous, even for a patient with dementia. I think, oh no you don't think, you did and you did it big. Gagging

35

Brenda Wojick

to death, I was finally able to mutter, "Well, what ever gave you that idea?" At this point I may have been clenching my teeth a bit, but in my head I was screaming, "it's up to your friggin' ear lobes, you are practically drowning in it, and apparently you can't swim because you only THINK you had a bowel movement?" My eyes were tearing up so bad from the smell, that the room was spinning. I felt like I might even fall unconscious. I'm done, dead on the floor. Can you picture the classic film *The Shining* with Jack Nicholson where he finally lost all self control? Do you remember the look in his eyes when he stated "Honey, I'm home!"? I sure as hell do. I became that insane sociopath- on the inside of course. There was no escape for me. Someone was going to have to get the smelling salts for me. How could one little itty bitty guy go so damn much, go so... Eeewww everywhere? I couldn't do this not one more time. No way, no how count me out.

The change of shift was coming, and it was like sweet music to my ears. It could be bad classical music for all I care. I was walking out into the hall to get some things to clean this guy up and the next nursing assistant came on shift, and she walked by me and asked me if I had any updates for her before I had left. "Hell yeah," I said. I walked by this poor girl, well, jogged is more like it, and forgive me, but all I could say to her was, "he needs to be cleaned. I THINK he had a bowel movement."

I've Got to Take a Dump

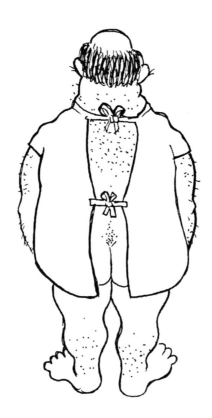

Since I am on the subject of doodie already, I want to continue on with some other fascinating stories, people and poop that I have encountered now that I finally made it as a nurse.

Brenda Wojick

When I start off my day, there is nothing better than walking down the hallway first thing in the morning ready to start my shift at 6:45 a.m. only to hear my patient yell out, "I've got to take a dump!" I heard him, the other nurses heard him, and every other patient on the floor heard him. There is not a cup of coffee big enough at that time of the day to prepare you for how your work day will be. You just know that it's going to be a bad one. I looked at one of my coworkers and asked her, "Did he just say I have to take a dump?" I didn't even wait for an answer, the question was rhetorical because I already knew the response. It doesn't take a rocket scientist to figure that one out. I'm shook my head in dismay whining to her like a baby, "Only me, this can only happen to me." I walked over to this gentleman's room, and I can't believe my eyes! Oh, my god, he is taking a poop on the floor. (I like the word poop) This is a 280 lb, grown man standing over his bedside taking a "dump"! I will spare you the gory, disgusting details, but I will tell you this, upon entering his room, his backside was facing me, and his Johnny was completely open, showing me and everyone else who passes by his room much more than we can handle. I had a front row seat to this show because his room was right in front of the nurse's station. My jaw dropped, and I think that may be an understatement because I think it actually hit the floor. I couldn't believe this. Someone, anyone pick my jaw up off the floor so that I can go into the room and rope off the crime scene. Perhaps rubbing his nose in his own shit would get my point across that shitting on the floor is a no- no in our hospital. I was thinking this may work, and he may never do it again after a good stern punishment. Then I wouldn't have to go through the hassle of interviewing for another job because I do not believe that the facility I work for would consider that quality patient care. Empathy went out the window as I stared at the steamy blob in the middle of the room wondering what the heck I was going to do with that pile. We don't keep pooper scoopers here.

As a nurse, it is my job to clean this man up, which I did slightly reluctantly because according to him, and using his words, "I can't wipe my own ass." There wasn't no sigh big enough for me to do at this point. I did it, I cleaned doody man up. I was just grossed out by the whole ordeal, so I couldn't help but just want to get out of this dude's room. He noticed my name tag and apparently thinking he was a funny man, he continuously repeated my name over and over and over yet again, "Brenda, Brenda, Brenda." He was finding this totally hilarious, but I was not amused to say the least. My eyeballs had to be bugging out my head by now. My friend Barbara always tells me, "You can tell exactly what you are thinking just by your facial expressions. You can't hide anything." I suppose this is right because I think at this point I felt my eyeball pop out of its socket and roll across the room. If this really could happen, I would pick it up and throw it at the guy. But anyway, I found this whole situation way too freaky, so I escaped out of that

Brenda Wojick

room immediately. I was like a fugitive on the loose. I wanted to change my name, my hours of work, and even my profession. I wanted to cut my hair and change my name just so I didn't ever have to go back in there again.

I decided to go on about my business, check my charts, and do some paperwork, when I realized I had to do my rounds again. I walked by his room again because he is still here, and I am still his nurse, and this guy is sitting in his chair, legs wide open, Johnny hiked up to his waistline exposing more than anyone in this hospital would care to see. **Side Note to all of the Men in the world**: the older you get the lower your balls hang, if you catch my drift; and it is not a glamorous site. They can actually hit the floor if you are not careful. He was now peeing all over the floor. This guy wasn't even attempting to make his way to the bathroom. Even better than attempting the bathroom, the little plastic urinal is sitting right next to him on the bedrail. Much to my dismay I made the slim attempt to solicit an answer. "Why are you urinating alllll overrrr the floooor?" I kept it cool on my outer shell, going crazy on the inside. He, with a big smirk on his face said, "I couldn't make it." I said, "make it where? Where do you have to make it? The urinal is right here, right next to you attached to your bed which is right next to the chair you are sitting in." I held the damn plastic thing up to his face. And with that smirk again from ear to ear he stated, "Oh, well." In my head I am trying to figure out how to push him in it. "Bill, do you

Can You Squeeze My Banana?

urinate on your floor at home?" "No." "Then why are you urinating on the floor here at the hospital?" I didn't even wait for an answer; I just walked out of the room chasing after my other eyeball that had popped out of the other socket. I had to tell someone about this, but you know what, anything goes and nothing at all is too shocking. We laugh it off as nurses. We can only laugh. What else can you really do? To this day I can still picture the creepy dude yelling, "I have to take a dump." Now, as if urinating and pooping on the floor wasn't despicable all by itself, due to the medicine that he was on for his urinary tract infection, Pyridium, his urine was bright orange. We actually have to warn our patients of this so that they do not become alarmed when they go wee wee. He unquestionably lied to my face when I asked him if he urinated on the floor before. I could see the orange trail of pee all over the place. He still had one last creepy laugh in the end when he poured salt in my wound. Thank the lord above that the local ambulance company came to get him to transfer him to a rehab facility, when one of the driver's said to me as he was leaving, "I think he left you a present in the corner." There it was- a bright orange puddle of pee --- housekeeping!!!

Good Catch

No secret, I am the queen of BM's (Bowel Movements). Everyone knows this, I know it, my fellow nurses now it, my friends and even the doctors know this. Doody patrol. It is sort of an ongoing joke on my floor because I do happen, just by luck, get the all the patients who continuously have BM's, large and small, all shapes and sizes, throughout the day. Just for the record, I will never ever get used to the smell that comes with doody patrol. People often say, "Oh, you get used to it" No, you don't. A smell is a smell is a smell, and a gross smell is even worse than a regular smell. I can't even get used to my own smell for crying out loud, let alone someone else's. I have gone into rooms with a mask on hoping it would help. I have on occasion had to excuse myself from a room because the vomit was right in my throat. Wearing the mask beats throwing up all over the sick patient though. Here's a thought for you: little babies, little diapers, little cute poopsies, big people, huge diapers, and enormous doodies. Not one of the finer aspects of being a registered nurse, could you tell?

Can You Squeeze My Banana?

I have this one friend of mine that is a clinical associate. Her name is Kim, and when we go into rooms together to change the patients, oh my god, some days I just have to say….well, you can imagine what I say. We grab the masks and attempt to make the best of a bad situation. I'm going in…go, go, go. It reminds me of the SWAT team, let's get in, get the job done and get out, do not say inside any longer than you have to. It would be awesome if the hospital had a team on the floor that was called in to only deal with bowel movements. If anyone were to stand outside of the door you would hear uh hum, uh hum, eeeehhhh hum that would be Kim and I clearing our throats at least 20 times to try and smother the smell. This technique doesn't work at all; it just makes a whole lot of noise and ultimately bothers your throat to no end. "Oh god, just make it go away."

Surprise, surprise, it was another day on the crazy floor. Each and every day it feels a little bit more like the psych floor that I never in a million years ever wanted to work on! Today, much like any other day, I was assigned to work with a cute little 78 year old gentleman, handsome, well groomed man, but guess what, he had dementia. This was going to be fun, fun, fun.

Screaming just two doors down the hallway was my 98 year old female patient who was ripping out her IV line, blood is oozing everywhere, and she is bright eyed and bushy tailed much like a rabid cat ready to rumble. First I ran into the room to calm her down, and

43

Brenda Wojick

she was venomously screaming that I was a demon, and she would not let me touch her or escort her back into bed. It was only 7:45 am, I'd been here for a whole 45 minutes. I only had roughly 7 more hours to go! Yay, lucky me.

Well, my little guy down the hall had to have a bowel movement. By now, this should not surprise you. I very much wanted to be productive in the medical field, but I feel as if I am everyone's natural laxative. I seem to get all of the shitty patients (No pun intended). Anyway, my patient stated that he was done and he couldn't go. Knowing that he was demented, I asked for assistance from another coworker to help me walk him back to bed. I snapped on the gloves, grabbed the facecloths and got ready to wipe his butt. I will never, even until this day, go in a room with a straight face on when I have to help the elderly by wiping their saggy little ass. It just doesn't happen. I will never get used to this no matter how long I remain in the nursing profession. So I was standing with my hand underneath him, and as I looked away into the toilet to see if he had left me any presents, when something hard and heavy fell right into the palm of my hand. Oh no he didn't....yes, he did! Icky! Gross! Apparently, he decided to let it go as we stood him up. Low and behold I held my hand up facecloth and all and said to the other nurse, "Look, a kaka ball," and the two of us could not stop laughing. The only words that this other nurse could mutter were "nice catch." I mean how, do you really respond to the moment when your patient drops a baseball

Can You Squeeze My Banana?

size kaka ball into your hand and he doesn't even know it? Well, I guess I'll carry on, but only after I plop it into the toilet bowl, wash my hands then sanitize my hands, and then wash them again.

Call the Freakin News

Karen, who is my BFFL, is also a fantastic nurse who taught me the soup to nuts of nursing. If it weren't for her, I would have never been able to cope with the beginning of my nursing career. I had a young female in her mid forties for a patient one day, and one day is just about all I could really take of her. She had a total hip replacement which is quite painful from what I understand. I wouldn't know because my hips are just fine. She was on a PCA pump which essentially a bag of morphine that is hung, and it is locked in a box so it cannot be tampered with. It is hooked up with your IV fluids and runs right into your IV site. This will then provide a certain amount of morphine roughly every 7 minutes should the patient need just by the click of a button. It does not provide with you any more medication than the doctor orders for and the pump is set for by the nurse. Morphine, that miracle drug, lowers your blood pressure and respirations, so when you are on a morphine pump, bed rest is the best remedy. Well, she was a smoker, and guess who was having nicotine fit, nicotine frenzy is more like it. She was out straight!

Can You Squeeze My Banana?

I had never seen anyone this crazy about a cigarette. She was borderline lunatic. She wanted a smoking pass so that she could go outside and smoke her ciggie butts when she felt like it, but the woman was on so much medication that as nurses, Karen and I felt that she should not go out for a butt, her blood pressure was like 80/40 which is very low, she was on the pump, and oh, did I mention that she was bleeding quite substantially from her incision site most likely from her determination to go smoke she was attempting to lift herself out of bed.

Now, this woman adds tears to her frustration so that the whole floor can hear her sobs. BBBooooooo Hooooooooo. Sniffle sniffle. Hoonnkk -that would be her blowing her schnozzle. I am absolutely perturbed by the entire situation and as a nurse. I'm sure you've encountered someone who is having nicotine fit in your lifetime, and if you haven't you ain't seen nothin' yet. Every problem in the entire world that she can think of becomes your fault, not theirs. The entire world just sucks because they can't smoke. Her elderly mother even came out of the room to bawl at us, and she even shouted to us that we should just give her a cigarette. Yeah, let me spark that puppy up on our respiratory floor that will go over quite well with our respiratory compromised patient's that we are attempting to keep alive. I got to tell ya, we are a funny little community we actually promote health and wellness here. Gees Louise.

She is now sniveling like she just lost her entire family. Sobbing is more like it. She is in such a frenzy she starts dialing the operator for

Brenda Wojick

the hospital asking them to help her. Unless she needs to make a long distance phone call calling the operator is not going to help. She's calling supervisors and also threatening to call News 7 because she has some sort of "connection" there. Can you imagine the breaking news on that story? "PATIENT AT LOCAL HOSPITAL DENIED SMOKING PASS"

This just in, a forty four year old female status post major hip reconstructive surgery is simply denied a smoking pass. She can't walk, she can barely talk due to the morphine pump, her blood pressure is in the toilet folks, it's up to a mere 80/40 and her incision site is bleeding quite heavily saturating the entire dressing on her leg. She is at this time demanding that a staff nurse transfer her to the wheelchair and wheels her out for a cigarette folks. The nurses on that floor will not do it. Can you believe this! They would rather make sure the patient is actually safe! We have never heard of such a thing. We will keep you updated on the story as more details are made available. Now back to you Jack!

Now, I would have loved for her to call her "connection" and have something such as that put on the news, that's true entertainment. Karen and I are completely baffled. She is so out of control, now she had her mother involved with the whole situation. Can you bitch slap a patient to knock some sense into her??? Nah, just joking, I know how unethical that is, but nothing in the books state that I can't dream of it. It would be a nice order for the physician's to write, ONE BITCH SLAP QID (four times a day) and if really out of control, TWO BITCH SLAPS PRN (as needed).

Down the hall we hear a commotion. She is screaming at the physical therapist that no longer works for our hospital, gee, I wonder

Can You Squeeze My Banana?

why. Somehow she gets this guy involved in the battle for nicotine. She's furious because he hasn't been by to get her up yet. The poor guy is mortified. He does eventually get her up into a wheelchair, and I page the doctor to explain to him the whole situation. After all of the arguing and hassling, the doctor decides to grant her a smoking pass after all. Who is crazier in this instance, her or the doctor? Maybe her oxygen level won't drop anymore after she starts puffing on the butts. Whatever! She may look good in a blue/gray skin tone. Maybe she'll be okay when she comes back in because I refused to take her down. Can you imagine????

Eyes as Big as Dinner Plates

"First the doctor told me the good news: I was going to have a disease named after me."
Steve Martin

Her eyes were as wide as dinner plates it felt like you could hear them tink when she blinked. I had never seen pupils so largely dilated, and her speech slurred with every word she attempted to utter from her toothless mouth. She was a very young woman in her early fifties who was admitted for a "car accident"; actually it was more like she wouldn't leave! She came well prepared for her stay and even brought along her own neck brace because she knew that the hospital would not be providing one for her. This is a nurse's dream patient who comes fully prepared with her own apparatus. Who the hell in their right mind does this sort of thing? The people who know how to play the system, that's who. This particular female was on so many pain pills, anti-depressants and anti-anxieties that she could barely keep her head up most times. She slept in the bed with her own T-shirt and a pair of white bloomers.

Can You Squeeze My Banana?

She knew right down to the millisecond when she was to receive each and every teeny weenie little pill that the doctors had ordered for her. She would ring the call bell, tell you she was in pain, summons me for her pill and then slump right back over again. Apparently the reason why she was in so much pain was because she was a RECOVERING quadraplegic. How in god's name do you recover from being paralyzed from the waist down? You may see an involuntary twitch or two, nothing to shake a stick at, but you don't recover, but she insisted. She had a story for everything about her, about her husband, about her pain pills, everything. Her husband, get this, was a physiotherapist and a neurologist who was also a paraplegic. What are the freakin' odds of that? I would have thought that with all of that money, he might have bought this lady a set of teeth considering she had no teeth, not even one in her head what-so-ever. Now, I would think that with her husband being a very important being in this world, they would have enough money to at least buy some of that shit. Apparently, they didn't have any food either because she was storing everything from her meals into a nice little plastic belonging bag for a rainy day. My other guess was that it was for the road when she left. She talked about her husband with great pride and honor, and then she slid in there that he was about 25 years older, and a quadriplegic.

On the day of discharge, he came up to get her in his wheelchair and all with some elderly gentleman probably older than the dirt he should

Brenda Wojick

be buried in, pushing him in the wheelchair. The patient told me that it was her father. Ewww, he was as old as her husband, both of them teetering on the edge of death with one foot in the grave. They entered the room and the physiotherapist/neurologist/bullshit artist parked his wheelchair at the foot of the bed, locked the wheels, and like Jesus walking on water, Moses parted the Red Sea for him, he got up from the chair, walked to the side of the bed and plunged his tongue into her mouth. I actually threw up a little bit in my mouth. Gross! I was barely able to contain my surprise, "I thought he was a quadriplegic," I blurted out and pointed to her husband at the same time. "Oh, he's recovered from that," she slurred at me with little spittle's flying across the room, as if there was nothing wrong. He must be a damn good neurologist because he has cured himself. Alleluia, you are healed! Now if I could only smack him on the forehead. If they had a cure for kleptomania we would be in business because as the old man pushed the other old man out, transport wheeled her away as she stuffed all of our linens into a bag and took them home with her. I guess the neurologist job doesn't pay that well.

Asthma or Addiction

For the absolute longest time when I became a nurse at this facility I felt as though I was being hazed. To me every assignment felt like I picked the short straw out of the pile yet again. Every patient I came in contact with had an outrageous story behind their hospitalization. As a new nurse I wanted to be empathetic and compassionate all the time giving everyone the benefit of the doubt. I know now that this rule definitely does not apply to everyone.

After I was through with my orientation with Karen, I was on my own, which is a scary situation. In nursing school you get ½ a patient, pick your half, and you give Tylenol out all the time. There are more back rubs given out on any given floor when there are student nurses around. This is what we do because we do not know how to do anything else. Now I had five patients and morphine to give. Nuts!!! I had a couple of young girls on my patient assignment for the day, and by young I mean twenties and thirties. One of the girls was down in room 07. She appeared to be "normal" enough, and I emphasize the word appeared,

Brenda Wojick

and by definition *normal (conforming to the standard or common type, regular, natural)* (3) this is who I assumed I would be dealing with today. Her diagnosis was asthma exacerbation, easy, right? NOT! Her diagnosis was anything but that.

She had a boyfriend that was at least 10 years older that her, and he hung out in her room constantly as if it were her own apartment. He only left her side briefly, and at first I thought, awww how nice, cute couple, then I realized that they were the devil's spawn.

She did seem to be very sick to me, hardly able to breathe, gasping for air, red faced and shaking. Her nostrils were in a flair. She kept ringing to tell me that she wasn't feeling good, and "Please get me some medication." Now for asthma there is only so much medication that you can give to help with an asthma attack or exacerbation, but she is looking for pain killers, you know, narcotics. I was new, and I was trying to work my routine, to get a feel for how I handled patients and their situations. I was thinking to myself why the hell does she need pain killers? Her chest hurt from coughing understandably so, but hell she didn't cough her lung up on the floor. I read her chart only to discover that she is former drug user. *Mayday! Mayday! Red Alert.* This could put a whole new spin on her hospitalization. As a nurse or a doctor you really try to avoid giving a former drug user drugs.

Her boyfriend was now frantically paging me into her room. The patient was very naked on the toilet, and they are both screaming that she can't breathe. In my nursing classes I did learn that if you can scream and yell at your nurse, you can breathe. I didn't see the universal sign for choking, therefore I assessed she was still breathing. I'm new, professional and not used to this sort of thing by any means. I start looking to everyone, especially Karen for advice, but further into her visit I didn't need that advice, I needed to have the DEA present. The whole time she was screaming, red faced, and then she started to projectile vomit everywhere. Now she needed a medication to stop the vomiting. This was her answer to every issue, "get me some medication."

Knock, knock, knock. That was me knocking on the patient's door which was shut and practically barricaded. Like the SWAT team I stepped back about 30 feet, and I ran with all my might. With my right shoulder I slammed up against the door with awesome force in attempt to get those people out. Nah, it just sounds so good. Eventually, I did get into the room though, and I noticed that the patient was resting comfortably in her bed as if she were passed out. She was too. Minutes before she was screaming for me, begging for pain medication and her face was reddened with such anger. The bathroom door was shut, but the light was on. I knocked on the door, and I could hear the boyfriend in there fiddling around. I knocked again, no answer. I jiggled the handle because now this situation was getting suspicious. I could hear banging, clanking and all kinds of shit going on in there. I told him to open the

Brenda Wojick

door or I was calling security. That door flung open. He said he had to go and like Flash Gordon he was off in a jiffy. I peered down, and the toilet was clogged with so many brown paper towels you couldn't flush the chain. Like a good little detective that I am, all because I watched the movie *SWAT*, I noticed one of the ceiling tiles had been moved, and there was toilet paper everywhere. I went over to check on the patient, and as I got closer to her, I noticed her left hand had very little tiny puncture holes in them, four to be exact, and the blood drops on them were fresh. The bitch was practically comatose. I thought this shit only happened in the movies. She, well he, was shooting heroin into her. She was withdrawing and needed a quick fix. There was no asthma attack. Lucky for her she did have asthma and that originally brought her into the hospital, but then she ended up withdrawing while she was here. Like a good boyfriend, he brought her in some vein candy and helped her get by those nasty episodes of withdrawal. He even left his spoon behind on the window sill.

"Does anyone have any advice for this situation for me?" I hollered down the corridor. I saw Karen and Kathy (one of our other veteran nurses) and immediately went to the two of them and rattled off my story. I couldn't tell if they were surprised or not. They both had been nurses for some time now, and maybe I was a naive nurse and just never realized these stupid ass things can occur right under my nose. I called the MD and his resolution was to move her closer to the nurse's station. I am not a babysitter.

Needless to say the entire afternoon was a fiasco. The girl's mother called the desk and demanded to speak with me, so I chatted with her. Her answer to the whole situation, and I do quote: "You nurses use your own stuff from the hospital anyway, so what makes this any different?" Way to go mommy. Is this chick for real?

I had security down there, the doctor, myself, other nurses and everybody that I could get my hands on involved. I had to ask the question, "Where do you look up a policy for shooting up heroin in your room and what to do with the spoon and needle when through?" All said and done, she did leave the hospital against medical advice. For some reason, I didn't think that she was going to follow our advice anyway.

Falling Rectum

"Be suspicious of any doctor who tries to take
your temperature with his finger."
David Letterman

"I'm having such a bad day," Sandy mentioned to me as I ran into her at the cafeteria. Sandy is the sweetest person you'll ever want to meet (besides my friends on my floor, Karen, Lois and Barbara, when Barb was with us) and funny beyond belief. To make you laugh is part of her job, and I would like to think that it is my place in the world as well. I gave her a great big hug and started to grab my Diet Coke with lime, pretty much this is all I had time for.

"Life sucks and then you die," Sandy snickered, "that's the kind of day it is."

"I take it that you are having a bad day on your floor," I asked. Sandy just rolled her eyes.

Then I whispered into Sandy's ear, "Sandy, my patient's rectum fell out today, how's that for a bad day?"

Can You Squeeze My Banana?

She was in hysterics. "Oh, my god, she really lost her rectum? Guess my day isn't so bad after all. I still have my rectum back there."

"Sandy," I replied, " I didn't even know a rectum could fall out."

For those of you who didn't realize this tidbit of information, it looks like a gigantic sausage link. It is not just a hole like people assume. It is actually muscle, a very ugly muscle. As you get older, beware because it can fall out without warning.

This particular female patient was the ripe age of 82, and she was slightly cuckoo, if you know what I mean. She was a tiny little thing, frail as she lay in bed, but her hair was nicely done, almost a reddish color, and she had fingernails the size of Freddy Krueger's daggers. Those were not well kept, thick and gross actually. I didn't realize that they would become deadly weapons in just a few hours. Poor thing had been stuck in bed, but what she really needed was to go to a rehabilitation center. Many of our patients should go to rehab, but somehow most of these elderly patients become our children, and they tend leave home and keep coming back. Our acute care floor was beginning to resemble a long term care nursing facility. She was on her extended stay here with us and physical therapy was here to get her up. Best thing for this little ole' thing, get movin', promote rehab, and ewww cut those fingernails…. I was at the nurse's station when I saw my patient, a physical therapist and one of the nurse's assistants walking with her in the hallway. Never say never around here, because never almost always

Brenda Wojick

does happen! Sha nay nay (changed name to protect the innocent) came up to me as I was attempting, only attempting the impossible, to do my paperwork, she had her hand on her head and that look of disgust on her face, but yet she was slightly grinning, "she just crapped all the way up the hallway." "What," I peeked out to see this for myself. "She just shit the whole way down the hall as physical therapy was walking her. It's everywhere, all over her, all over the floor." I started for the hallway where house keeping was putting out signs, CAUTION, WET FLOOR, and quickly she was being whisked into her room, and towels were everywhere. We need signs that say SHIT ON FLOOR. We seem to have more shit on the floor than water. "She's definitely gonna need a shower," Sha nay nay was saying, and I agreed, ya think? Until then we decided to put her in the bathroom to finish her duty, and this would allow us to set up the shower. This is where the massacre took place in the tiny little 4X6 white, bathroom.

Remember I told you about those daggers that my little charming lady had, oh yeah; she decided to use those blades on herself. I knocked on the bathroom door to check in on her, and when I entered, oh my god, it was a crime scene! I thought we needed a forensics team down here, CSI, anybody. There was blood and poop everywhere. "What are you doing" I calmly attempted to ask my patient as she was apparently elbow deep into her rectum. I kid you not she had one arm, the other arm was missing, that's how far up her ass she had it. She was the one arm bandit, "I'm pushing my hemorrhoids back up there," she told me. "You are what," I yelped very panicky. "Honey, your fingernails are so long, you will hurt yourself and damage your insides. Please, don't do that." I begged this little woman. She just told me, "I have to, they are falling out." She was wiping her hands everywhere and anywhere and the white walls were no longer. "Sha nay nay, we need to get her in the shower. She's done. I'm done."

The girls got her into the shower across the hall, and once again I was going to attempt to get some paperwork finished so that I would not have to stay late that day. Did I really think that this was going to happen? Not in the real world.

"Come quick," Catherine yelled to me. "There's something that is protruding from her buttocks and it ain't a hemorrhoid." "What," I said as I jumped to my feet and sprinted down the hallway. I reached the shower stall to find a wrinkled hunched over little old lady "Honey, turn around," I said to my patient as the girls were washing her up, "turn around and bend over, I need to look at your bum." (A pay increase would be nice right about now) "Wholly crap, was all I could say." Her rectum was falling out, literally. The muscle was protruding farther than I ever thought possible. I had to grab the doctor for this one. I had never seen anything like this before. I got the MD to come down and take a look at this for me to see how to handle this.

Brenda Wojick

Not touching the sausage link that was hanging from her ass, I put my little lady back into bed and explained to her what was going on. How do you explain this delicately? "Dear, your rectum is falling out. You need to stay in bed, and please do not move for a while." My what..., what's going on? Guurrrlllll, she had no idea what is going on. "Your rectum is...Ah, your bum is falling out." My what, my bum?" Let me tell you those are not hemorrhoids that you have been trying to push back in, as you would call it." "Well, what do you mean?" I mean your bum is falling out, don't touch it, don't move. You will need to stay in bed. Legs up on the pillow my dear." I really do hope Sandy is having a much better day than this....

Dura Man

Look, up in the sky…it's a bird; it's a plane…its duragesic man.

Definition – duragesic patch – it delivers a potent narcotic painkiller for a period of three days. They are prescribed for chronic pain relief when short acting narcotics fail to provide relief.

A person who is wearing a duragesic patch should wear one, and only one at a time. It is worn when a person has chronic pain that isn't always relieved by other medications. It is a thin square patch much like the Nicotine patch that is out there on the market. You wear it for a certain amount of time; you remove it, wash your skin, and then apply a new clean one. Not really that hard to understand and do. They do run out of medication after that certain amount of time. 72 hours people. It's not like an endless supply of narcotics that you stick on and have relief for the rest of eternity. It releases the contents into your skin over time. You won't be getting high on this puppy.

I got an admission one particular day, a gentleman in his forties, admitted here before, this time for pneumonia. He got to the floor, and

Brenda Wojick

he's walky, he's talky, and he definitely did not want to be here. His wife made him come, he informed me. I can't imagine what he was doing here because he only smoked about 3 packs of cigarettes a day, so where that silly pneumonia he has came from just baffled me.

Tony did not want to talk to me when he hit the floor. He wanted a cigarette. He wanted to walk off the floor and have a cigarette. God this blows my mind when people are this stupid. He had refused all care until he got this butt. He was sweating; he was agitated and yelling about his cigarette. No explanation was good enough for him as to why he couldn't go out this minute. Well, he won- he got to have his cigarette. The doc's were not that hard on the patient's before the hospital became a nonsmoking facility. Whateva! How much worse can the pneumonia get in the next five minutes right? Actually, maybe the cigarette will get rid of the expiratory wheezes that he has throughout his entire chest wall. It sounds like a damn saw cutting through wood when he breaths, but far be it for me to judge.

He comes back to the floor, finally and allows me to fully assess him. As a nurse I do a head to toe assessment from mental status right down to what a person's skin looks like. It also includes an interview in regards to the person's health. We get to the chronic pain part, and he tells me that he is on the duragesic patch. "So where exactly do you have the patch," I asked him. Simple question or so I thought. A lot of people who have back pain keep it on their backside on the area that hurts. His

Can You Squeeze My Banana?

response to me is, "all over." "I think you misunderstood me, I know your pain is all over, but where exactly on your person do you keep the patch so when I have to replace it I know where to put it?" "All over myself." He says. I'm baffled now, but won't be for long. He lifts his shirt for me and there are like 52 patches scattered all over him. Not really, but he's covered with patches from the base of his neck to the waist of his pants, and where there are not any patches there are grungy dirt marks from where the old ones were at one time. He had 8 patches on him and about 10-12 dirty rings around him. He was proud; he was standing up showing me his patches and how he put them everywhere. "I keep six of them on at a time." He says. The dude resembles a checkerboard. "You do know that you can remove the old patches, don't you? The medicine in them is only good for 72 hours, then you do not need it any more." "I need them all on, they help me," he said. I was makin' the reach in to attempt the removal of one of them. He back away so quickly, that wasn't going to happen.

Drive By

It was like a rumbling explosion that took me completely by surprise. This particular day I was having a "good" day, a "quiet" day on the floor, and the nursing assistant that I was working with was great, the patients were great, and who could ask for anything else more. This never happens. We never say the "Q" word because if you believe in superstitious encounters as I do never say quiet because your whole day turns to hell with a capital H. Today I was working down in the "hole" which meant that I had the patients down at the very end of the hallway. There are roughly four patient rooms down there, so I had the patient that was in the very last room on the left. This room is always the bad luck room based on the many experiences I have managed to survive while being the nurse assigned to that room. Today it was a female who had a multitude of health problems, and to put it in frank nonmedical lingo, she had tubes from every orifice imaginable including Foley catheters, rectal catheters, tracheotomy tubing, oozing mucus, restraints on her wrists because she had dementia and was pulling at those tubes,

Can You Squeeze My Banana?

skin ulcers, multiple IV lines and much more. You get the picture? Well, moving right along Rolanda and I had to get this patient changed, and she had a Stage IV ulcer on her coccyx area that needed a little TLC along with the soiled depends that she had on. "Code brown, we have a Code Brown" Boy I love that one. My major in nursing school should have been shit removal. I feel like superman with a big S on my shirt, and the S does not stand for superwoman either. Now, this patient has many infections, from MRSA (Methicillin Resistant Staph Aureus) to C-Diff (which is an infection in your poop) so to start out with, we look like a ridiculous Hazmat duo approaching the room with our yellow gowns, face shield, gloves and so on! It's a good thing we did because we were entering, "the war zone"! The unresponsive patient is dead weight, and we can tell that she is a volcano ready to erupt. You can just sense this, and oh, by the way, you can hear her stomach rumble. Someone from up above was watching over us today, AMEN!

We rolled our patient over, dead weight and all, as gently as we could. The incredible noise from her ass was so loud, so long, so gross... The two of us were stunned and could only laugh and a snort may have followed as well. I mean what do you do? Well hell, I did jump out of the way to dodge the bullet. It sounded like a machine gun going off and if anything was going to fly, it wasn't going to fly on me. I jumped to the side so fast I tripped and hit the wall behind me. We were laughing hysterically, and we must have looked like two of the biggest idiots.

Brenda Wojick

This poor woman didn't even realize she was doing this, unfortunately, she was barely conscious at this point, but boy could she let one rip. "Rolanda, I think we were just involved in a drive by!"

Nasty Girl

I wipe my butt, do you wipe yours??? Now, I am sure that you are wondering why the hell I am asking this twisted question. No one should be embarrassed by this, because the truth of the matter is that we all do, male, female, young or old, at some point have to wipe our butts, right? Mother Nature calls upon us at some point to drop the kids in the pool, if you will, and wipe when we are done. If you find work in that special career such as the one that I chose, you too will have the golden privilege and honor to wipe other people's butts. How exciting!!

Next question to ponder… why wouldn't a person wipe their own butt after using the facilities? Does your hand not reach that far back? Is it difficult for one to assume the proper position to perform such a task? Can you not bend over that far? I would imagine, and this is just a guess, that one might feel a "cling on" sensation on the derriere region which would then induce a hopeful desire to shake it off your back door. Shake it, flick it, pick it whatever your desire, but your instinct will tell you to get rid of it.

Brenda Wojick

As you are reading this please don't wince in disgust. While I am pretty certain that you are nauseated by this topic, there isn't a human being out there that hasn't done this. I just happen to be the individual that is willing and able to write about it. One can also tell if we have not, shall we say, wiped well enough. I am talking skid marks people, tire tracks in the underwear. I might add that this is more prevalent in males than females, but any hoo…

How lazy can one person be when all the signs are there, and yet you still ignore the "wiping criteria"? Do we really need a manual on how to wipe your ass properly? This particular female patient of mine was a sweet woman in her late sixties- somewhat obese, but she was lying in bed looking quite healthy. Mary had just come back from surgery, which left her with two enormous gaping holes on either side of her rectum, all because she didn't wipe her butt. Wasn't that part of Mary's potty training class many moons before? I don't know about you, but I would have definitely made the effort even if it required a little bit of contortion maneuvers to get my body in a good position to do so. It beats the hell out of going to surgery to remove a good portion of your ass tissue.

Don't be jealous, but my job as Florence Nightingale is to pack those gaping holes with sterile gauze so that they can heal from the inside out. It was quite painful for the patient, quite abhorrent for me if I don't mind saying so. Wads of tissue were exposed as well as what looked like chicken skin. It appeared as if there were a tunnel from one side to the other but the rectum was in the way. I could not and would not want to image how painful this entire experience has been for this woman. Unfortunately it didn't just end when the surgery was complete, oh no! There was no wiping butt now that there were two gaping holes on either side, so the alternate measure was to take a sitz bath every time she had a bowel movement. I would be so constipated because of the fear that I would have of pooping. I would hide the poo poo forever and ever inside of me. Think of the body's natural reaction when you have to do NUMBER 2. Your sphincter muscle kicks in and sends a contracting reaction to the anus and rectum that says push and squeeze and let it go. Now, if you were missing fat folds on the sides of your rectum, would you want to push, squeeze and let go? Better yet, now when you have to go you must sit on a bed pan that has water swirling around in it to clean the inside of your raw wounds. I had to pack the wounds with almost a foot of gauze on each side. Not fun people. It was bad for Mary too.

Riddle: How do you have a bowel movement?

Answer: Very carefully. Wouldn't it have been a lot easier to wipe your butt?

Giving Birth (or sort of)

Of course it was the change of shift and something was going very wrong with one of my patients. One of the nursing assistants came to me at 3:10 pm to let me know that there was blood coming from my patient's rectum. Oh boy, this should be a good one. What's another hour at work? I went to assess the situation, and this poor guy, who only had one leg, was bleeding from his rectum. No, scratch that. He was giving birth from his rectum. This story may turn your stomach, so do not say I didn't warn you. He was passing clots the size of placentas. Yes, placentas. I can remember my cat giving birth to kittens, and they come in a sack that the mother cat has to clean off. This is what I was picturing as I watched this patient. I thought I might save it for the MD to take a peek at. He should enjoy this one. I had never seen clots so big come from some place where they shouldn't be coming from.

"Has this ever happened to you before," I ask.

"No," he replies, "but I've had hemorrhoids before."

Can You Squeeze My Banana?

I wanted to say, "Dude, this isn't a little blood from a tiny hemorrhoid. You now have a son, Peter the placenta weighing in at 3 lbs. The damn thing was so big it was horrifying. It was the size of my head.

For those who are wondering, the gentleman was going to be fine, and we flushed Peter down the toilet. It was just one of those Enquirer stories I thought you would enjoy.

Ready my lips

Frustrated, Nah. Ironic, yes. I had a female patient admitted from the CCU (critical care unit) to my floor, and I was forewarned that this could be a difficult case to handle. This particular woman had a tracheotomy performed in the past for obvious respiratory reasons, and she did not have the cannula in place, she had the stoma which is the hole in her throat open to air. The reason for admission was respiratory distress. She was previously intubated and extubated. Well, this was a normal case for our floor, but the kicker of it all is she had MRSA in her sputum. MRSA is that I spoke about in a previous story. It is infection that can be found in your blood, wound and in this situation, her sputum, and it most definitely be transmitted. As "respiratory nurses" its second nature to us and it's a situation that we handle on an almost daily basis, so we have to take precautions when it is in the sputum or anywhere else for that matter. If thy cough, sputum will fly, so we wear these very attractive yellow gowns, masks and gloves for protection. Follow me here; the mask covers your mouth, right? Yes, it does. I went

Can You Squeeze My Banana?

in to speak to my patient and she was DEAF. Well, they told me that she read lips. Good! This should have helped me. So I did what every other normal person does to a deaf person- I went into her room and yelled really loud because now I'm sure that she will hear me! What an idiot I am. She was looking at me with this strange little expression on her face. Well, she was reading lips all right, right through my heavy blue tight fitted mask that was being used to protect me from the MRSA that was in her sputum. I obviously had the situation well under control. I was yelling at a deaf woman who was trying to read my lips through a mask that I had on to protect me from contracting an infection. So I called for assistance. Three nursing assistants showed up, and unless they knew sign language, I didn't know what the hell I was thinking. These are the days that you need to roll right back into bed and start all over again.

You Have the Right to be Laid to Rest

"I think the worst time to have a heart attack is during the game of charades…or a game of fake heart attack"
Demetri Martin

If I ever live to be 102, well let's just say that I hope I don't, but if I do, I want to make sure that my children or grandchildren only love me a little. This may sound bizarre and peculiar, but I will explain why. I once had a patient who was a cute little tiny itty bitty woman name Helen, and she was the young age of 102. That was astonishing for some people, as for me it was a little bit frightening. More power to you if you have the energy to live that long. Personally, once I start pooping my pants I want to become a DNR and quite possibly request the pillow treatment, if you know what I mean. I may even have that tattooed all over my body just to be on the safe side.

This little chickie poo lived with her granddaughter and that may not necessarily have been a good thing. At the very ripe ole' age of 102 lets face it, your days are numbered. There is no surprise, no secrets. At

Can You Squeeze My Banana?

some point you will only have two or three hours to live. Let's be realistic people. There is not a soul in the health care profession misleading you in any way on this one. You will not be expected to be with us for another 10 years, but there is always an exception to every rule. Apparently, her granddaughter had a hidden agenda. Instead of letting this fragile lost soul rest in peace, the granddaughter had her admitted to the hospital multiple times. She should have been allowed to pass peacefully in the night, instead she ended up at our hospital and had a G Tube inserted into her abdomen. The reason for this was that the patient was not eating well. A G tube is inserted into your stomach and allows you to receive nutritious feedings. Yum! My first response is *you have got to be kidding me*. As I explained to my friend, Lois, "She's full. She has been eating for over 100 hundred years, and she doesn't want to eat no more." Why was this so hard to comprehend? She could not open her eyes. If she couldn't do this simple little task, how the heck was she going to find her mouth and put food in it? Simple answer to this question, she wasn't. So the granddaughter opted for the invasive procedure to have them put a tube into her stomach so that she would receive nutrition. This was when she was 101. Side note to my husband and kids: DON'T EVER DO THIS TO ME! I will haunt you.

I knew I was in trouble when I had to take care of her, and I walked in one day and the granddaughter was in the room already. No one ever goes home to get any sleep around here. She said to me, "She doesn't

Brenda Wojick

look good to me today. How is she doing?" I'm thinking, *how the hell can you tell?* She looked the same as she did the day before; lying back with her eyes closed not uttering a word. I'm sure this wasn't much different from yesterday.. She's old as hell. The granddaughter did not like the care that we were providing her grandma. She said to me, and to other RN's on the floor, "You don't know how to do your job. Don't touch her at all. I am sending in a personal care taker to sit with her and take care of her." What is she going to do, just sit there and stare at the patient? She can watch the cobwebs form, and that's about it. There isn't a thing that anyone can do for this person. She could possibly sit and pray that this lady passes into heaven for her sake. I have compassion people, and observing patients sink into their own souls is not what I enjoy doing. Besides, another day with the granddaughter and I just might pass through the pearly gates myself.

The granddaughter continued, "I want to see the doctor because he's not doing his job." Dr. Rogers wasn't a miracle worker, he's a medical doctor. Dr. Kevorkian on the other hand, he is a miracle worker. This granddaughter reversed her grandmother's DNR status. Oh for Christ sakes. Was she smoking weed? When I came onto the floor that morning, the nurse told me she reversed her status. I think I nearly fell on the floor! Even the greatest legends Bob Hope and George Burns had to go at some time.

140 Beats per Minute

"If you die in an elevator, be sure to push the up button"

Jack Levenson

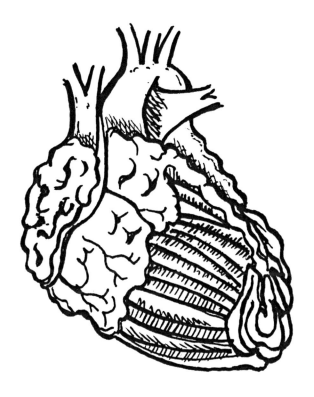

I had just experienced my first patient death, and since I had not been a nurse for long when this event took place, it got very interesting. In nursing school, as sadistic as it sounds, once you have your first death,

Brenda Wojick

it's over. You can now move on and handle anything else that comes your way.

It was New Years Eve 2005. This gentleman's death itself was very difficult because I had been caring for him for more than a week, and you tend to develop a rapport with not only the patient but the family as well. He was in his late 80's, and from what the family has told me he lived a very fulfilling life. I, on the other hand, saw my life flash before me as the events unfolded.

The day was like any other day on our floor, and I proceeded to make my rounds checking in on my patients passing out their medications. This particular man was not looking that well today. His temperature was low, and we could not really get an accurate oxygen saturation level on him because his extremities were so cold. I continued to monitor my patient that day. I made my way into his room to say hi, and his daughter was with him feeding him orange slices. I asked him how he was doing, and he started to answer me when all of a sudden he looked at me strangely, eyes wide as if he had seen a ghost. He turned a shade of gray that I had never seen on the color spectrum before, and made this god awful gurgling noise as if he choked on the orange As he went gray, I think it was at that point that the color drained from my body and I turned whiter than the sheets on the bed. The little voices in my head, which kept yelling *DON'T JUST STAND THERE*, were so loud I was certain everyone in the room could hear them. I wanted to

80

yell back at the creepy voices and say, "What do I do? What do I do?" The daughter touched my arm and asked if her father is going to be alright. All I could do was look at her with a tear in my eye. You see, although I was struggling on the inside, I am unruffled and composed on the outside which is the way it should be. I snap into action, and I remember that this gentleman is a Do Not Resuscitate, DNR. Whew! I never perspire, but I began to feel like a wet sponge. I attempted to feel for the patient's carotid artery, and oh, my god, it is beating at like 140 beats per minute. PANIC MODE. This couldn't be happening! He looked dead, he felt dead. I thought he was dead. Oh, wait, that was the pulse in my finger. I excuse myself from the room, and can only imagine what an idiot I sounded like when I frantically grabbed Karen's arm as I began to rattle off to her, "I need a second opinion." The two of us walked side by side as I was babbling off the specifics, "He is a DNR, but crap, I think he stopped breathing. I sure as hell can feel my pulse though." She immediately and very calmly came into the room with me and took the blood pressure. I was attempting to listen to his heart beat. Why was his heart beating at 140 beats per minute? He's dead! Again, apparently that's my heart that's beating, for crying out loud, my heart is actually in front of me. I can see my heart! I want to yell out and say, *Does anybody else see this? That's my heart and I'm ready to friggin pass out over here.*

81

Brenda Wojick

Unfortunately, it was his time, and he passed away. I really needed to go back to the nurse's station at this point because my knees were weak, my body was shaking, and I wanted to just throw up. I paged the Doc that was taking care of this gentleman to inform him of his passing so he could come down to the floor and pronounce his death. He went in and comes out a few minutes later and he must have forgotten that it was me who called him to inform him because he walks by me and says, "Is this your patient over there?" "Yes," I said. "There's a man on the floor," he said, and walked away. Now my mind was filling with crazy thoughts. Did he roll out of bed? Did he come back to life? Somebody work with me here. Not being inconspicuous at all I am now yelling, "Karen, Dr. Smarty pants over there said there's a man on the floor!" We both run over to the room expecting to find a corpse on the floor, and low and behold, the patient's grandson walked in and couldn't handle what he saw, and he hit the floor. I said to Karen, "who the heck is going to pick my sorry ass off the floor when I go down?" In the wise words of an old co-worker, it's just too much. Help me here and let this day be over and eventually it was, but not soon enough! I thank Karen for getting me through that day.

I'm going to continue on with this day because we all know there are eight hours in this shift, and it will only get better to say the least. It's on to the next patient of mine. The nursing assistant approaches me, "Brenda, the guy in 18 wants to know when he is going to get

Can You Squeeze My Banana?

his services today." "Services," I said with a chuckle. "What services is he looking for exactly?" If you think back to the beginning of the book when I provided you with a list of definitions and words, I guess providing services would fit in just nicely, it just sounds freaky. Are we talking church services, sexual services, and funeral services? What?

I went down and introduced myself as I always do, "my name is Brenda, and exactly what services can I provide for you today, sir?" You see, when a patient is grouchy or sarcastic, if you are just a little bit sarcastic back in a nice tone of voice, they catch your drift most of the time, and they will no longer be that way back to you. Most of the time it works and in this case it did. He was going to be all right. Well, all right in the tone of his voice sort of way, as for his left big toe that was another story. That big piggy had apparently went to the market, got sliced off by the roast beef cutter, and it ended up with all of the diabetic side effects reeking havoc on his big piggy. There would be no wee, wee, wee all the way home. His toe was pretty much going in the trash. Diabetes had most definitely gotten the best of this dude. There was an ulcer that presented on his toe that was going to be debrided today by one of our surgeons. I went and got everything prepared for the doctor, set it up at the bedside, and we were ready to rock and roll. Due to the patient's neuropathy, it was likely he could not feel a thing that the doc was doing to his toe. The more I think about it this is a good thing because by the time he was done debriding the infection, there was,

Brenda Wojick

oh, half a toe. Big piggy now resembled little piggy. EEEEWWWW! There was so much infection that I thought the doctor's scalpel was going to come right through the other side of his toe. "John, are you doing okay, are you in any pain?" I asked even though it sounds like the most ridiculous question ever. Apparently startled by my question, he groggily replied, "no." The dude was falling asleep through this procedure. He was losing most of his toe and he was off in happy, nappy land. I couldn't believe it. I would be slamming my head against the wall hoping to put myself out of my misery. I guess neuropathy can be a good thing, huh? I was probably experiencing more pain than he was from watching the whole darn procedure.

Hole in One

My little cute 93 year old patient was calling for me. Poor guy had prostate cancer, so as you can imagine he had a problem peeing. In this instance, his bladder would become full, and he then had to straight catheterize himself to get rid of the urine. His bladder was unable to empty on its own. This required placing a Foley catheter into his own pee pee head, which extends through the urethra into the bladder and it drains out the urine. It's like a giant straw. He usually did this on his own. I can't picture this at all, nor do I want to thank you very much. I found out I had a written order from the doctor to put a Foley catheter in him while he is at the hospital so he would not have to keep doing this himself. You would think that it's a one shot deal, can't miss the spot that the catheter goes into one hole and it's the only one in that general area, but as a nurse and looking back at previous situations, this could become a tricky little event, one that I wish I could have avoided, but hello, we are providing nursing care here.

Brenda Wojick

I got myself all prepared for the main event. I gathered all of the sterile equipment, and placed it at the bedside. I explained to the patient what I was doing. Please remember he was pretty familiar with the whole experience since he did this for himself. I attempt to grab his shriveled 93 year old penis which is almost obsolete at this point. He was not circumcised, so I had to uncover the top of the penis in order to insert this catheter. This required the rolling down of the foreskin (I'm sure, in fact, almost positive you have a visual at this time), and at this stage of life skin really has no recoil to it. There is no snapping it back into place. It is now saggy sad skin. Icky! Did I mention he is 93? I was thinking of my paycheck at the end of the week because what else could I possibly think of at a time like this when I hear, "aaahhhhh." I really hoped he wasn't aaaahhhing at me. I didn't think that a man of his age being almost a century old could actually feel anything. When I looked up he had a grin on his face from ear to ear! "OOOhhhhhh," he gurgled from the side of his mouth. Some days are just worse than others. I think this little dude thought it was our first date. I needed to just insert this Foley and get the heck out of that room. Maybe I should have gone into computer programming.

Boy or Girl?

"Talk about getting old. I was getting dressed and a peeping tom looked in the window, took a look and pulled down the shade"
Joan Rivers

Today was a good day to laugh. Today, we laughed, ha ha ha ha ha. That feels good. It cleansed the soul in a big way. I was thinking that it better be cleansed before my next patient got here. "Brenda, you're getting a transfer in 12," Barbara tells me with a smile. I miss Barb. She ended up getting another job somewhere else. Barb said, "This one is for you." My interest was definitely peaked by now. Like a little puppy dog, my ears were wide open, and my tail was waggin'. Give it to me baby.

"Okay, who is it," I ask.

Barb told me that she was a 53 year old female in for rule out MI, which is a heart attack, and oh yeah, SHE is a HE.

"What part of the gender do I get?" I can barely get the words out of my mouth. I am not naive, and I know what goes on in this outrageous scientific universe we live in, but I will never understand why, why

Brenda Wojick

people feel they need to change their gender, but who the heck am I to say, I am writing this crazy ass book, but on the other hand, I am not adding a penis onto my Va jay jay.

I got report from the ER nurse, and I found out that the person is presently a female who formerly was a male, just like the musician Prince is former known as Prince, and then he was a symbol who now is Prince again. Apparently she is 85% female. didn't want to know where and what the other 15% was where it was or what it looked like. These surgeries are becoming much more common in today's world. It's like asking do I wear the blue shirt or the red one. Do I wear my penis today or take it off?

The patient arrived on the floor via stretcher, and suddenly I became retarded. I tripped over my tongue, I couldn't get the words out of my mouth, and I was referring to HER as a HE most of the time. She is so manly that it is hard to say she. I felt like an idiot. I was feeling as tiny as the pink eraser on the head of a pencil, and right about this time, any of the human qualities I once retained resembled just about that, an eraser. .

Standing in front of me was a 6 foot female with a five o'clock shadow that resembled the same five o'clock shadow that Paul Cellucci, the former Lieutenant Governor of Massachusetts, sports. Man there was a lot of stubble there. It was like indoor outdoor carpeting on her face. And believe me there ain't enough base make up to hide that

Can You Squeeze My Banana?

stubble even if you robbed every damn drug store in Massachusetts. She had medium length gray hair that was just not becoming at all, caked make up on her face, fingers that resembled sausages and were painted in a death defying chocolate color, and an Adams apple so big it poked me in the eye as I entered the room. Like the old cliché, curiosity killed the cat, so I maintained my distance which is hard when you are a nurse and trying to perform your physical assessment. Her voice was deep, hence the Adams apple and the penis SHE was born with, and she stated that her voice is not usually this deep it's because she hasn't been feeling very well. She was attempting with every ounce of energy to clear her throat so that her voice would sound better, but given the fact that she went through puberty as a boy this could pose a problem. She could clear her throat a thousand times over and it would still not change a friggin' thing. It was most definitely a man's voice no matter what she does.

"Urinal or hat to urinate in," is what the nursing assistant asked the patient. I would never have been able to ask that question as outspoken as I am. I choked on my own spit. Oh no she didn't......Oh yeah she did......The patient replied, "I've had some work down there while waving at her lower abdominal - groin section. Who the hell has work done down there? I know people shave down there, and many people may get a Brazilian wax down there, but to say work down there sounds

Brenda Wojick

like you hopped on a creeper and rolled under the hood of a car for an oil change.

He said, "I use a hat" referring to the plastic thing that we place in the toilets for all patients so that we can keep count of their urine output. I couldn't believe he answered. Boy was this awkward. The plumbing was all wrong in this patient, and I am such a babbling idiot I couldn't even figure out where to begin to assess her…him. Head to toe I reminded myself, head to toe Bren. By the time I got to toe, she had the shoe size of a small tug boat. Holy molly I had the heebie jeebies. She took off her 1980 black flat style shoes and they were feet the size of …. I don't know what, a two foot sub sandwich perhaps. They were just big, and she had the same chocolate painted toenails. Brrrrrr. It sent chills down my spine. I wiped the back of my neck hoping I could persuade the hairs on my neck to get the hell down. She would actually walk in the hallways in her tight Johnny and her big ole shoes as they did a clippity clop down the hallway that sounded like a horse galloping. With the right hand flaccid and limp at the wrist, it truly was a pathetic sight but who am I to say, I was pathetic at this point in time, and I am sure that my face said it all, loud and clear. I never really got to see what was under the Johnny. She kept it tightly wrapped, and I really didn't want to see anymore. My eyes had seen enough. The end of my shift was coming, so I just basically had to settle her in. Needless to say, she was somewhat of a tourist attraction when she walked around our

Can You Squeeze My Banana?

hallway. People were gawking and with good reason. Her appearance was astonishing you just couldn't help but notice. It was like watching the monkeys at the zoo, you just had to stare, and when your mother tells you to come on she hasn't got all day, you still can't peel your eyes from those monkeys. We ended up finding out that she was actually removed from another local hospital and told never to come back. She was throwing her two foot shoes at people in the emergency room. Why don't we ever get to throw people out???

Help Me

"It's been a rough day. I got up this morning, put on a shirt, and a button fell off. I picked up my briefcase and the handle came off. I'm afraid to go to the bathroom."
Rodney Dangerfield

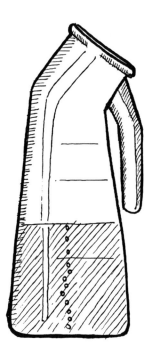

Keeping with the theme, my journey continues…could there be anything worse than touching a strange man's penis??? I don't think so…

Can You Squeeze My Banana?

"Good morning, any updates for me," I asked as I got to the nurse's station on a bright and sunny June morning. New day, new assignment, same old shit though. "How was the night?" I dared to ask the night shift nurse. "Well, it wasn't bad. There are a few needy patients that are on the call bell all night long. What else is new?" By the way, you have your bell ringers, and then you have your ball busters who just like to ring, and ring, and ring. You can easily decipher the two. At this time of the morning I'm only half awake, and my compassion for any individual does not kick in until after I've had my first cup of coffee so fill it up.

"The guy in 21 kept ringing all night, and it's rather strange because he would ask me if he could use his urinal, and he wanted me to position it into the urinal," the night nurse informed me while making a peculiar face.

"And he asked you to do this like all night? What the hell is wrong with his hands?" I just had to say with laughter in my voice. How did I know her reply would be, "nothing, absolutely nothing." It was sort of a rhetorical question because it did not require any type of answer. She was so funny telling the story because she spoke with an awesome English accent. She proceeded to tell us that it was like grabbing the back side of a cat's neck and that is how she grabbed a hold of his penis, and then flopped it in the urinal, although it was not as cute and fuzzy as a kitty cat. He wouldn't even help her in any way. He just lay there still as a stump.

Brenda Wojick

"Oh, hell no he won't pull that crap with me," I responded. "He'll be doing his own penis handling."

At each patient's bedside we have white communication boards. I wish I could have added this on his communication board: *No Pee Pee Playing, Poking or Pushing, have a nice day.* In his chart I noticed that he was only 57, 5-7 years old. Although he'd had hip and shoulder surgery, I didn't see anything at all in that chart about hand, wrist, finger or dinky surgery. This dude needed to buy a vowel, get a clue and realize what a nurse's role actually is. We, referring to nurses and nursing assistants, are in no way, shape or form personal penis chaperones, and for all intent and purposes, I don't even like touching my cats by the back of the neck, so there!

I was all fired up when I noticed that he was ringing his call bell. I cracked my knuckles, twisted my neck, and bent my back. I was ready, and I was going in. "Good morning Ralph, my name is Brenda, and I am going to be your nurse today. How can I help you?" In a weird sort of intoxicated voice, the gentleman said to me, "I need to use the urinal." "No problem," I replied as I handed it to him.

"I can't hold it, you need to do it," he said to me.

"Ralph, I think you can do it. C'mon, you're a young guy, and there's no reason why you cannot hold a urinal on your own." I handed him the urinal and he proceeded to pull down his covers. "Position it for me," he muttered.

Can You Squeeze My Banana?

He was going to see me position my hands on my hips as I turned around and walked out the door. Please understand that I consider myself to be a kind nurse, but there is no reason what so ever that this man could not do this himself. A line had to be drawn somewhere, and This situation had gotten past the point of obscene. Some people think that you will do anything for them because they are in the hospital, but that was definitely not the case. Lines have to be drawn very clearly for some patients and this was one of those times.

"What in the world do you do when you are home," I asked.

There was no reply from the sad little man who lay before me.

"Here's your urinal, ring when you are done," I said. How much easier could it get for this guy, for any guy really? It requires no effort at all and you don't even have to open your eyes if you don't want to, for crying out loud. Lift it, position it, and drop it in.

I was hoping that he would realize the deal eventually.. Here was a 57 year old gentleman who missing the big toe on his right foot, and the toe next to it was not so pretty either, due to diabetes. I went into his room to check on him and he was shoveling a Boston Cream donut that his wife brought him from Dunkin Donuts into his mouth.

I wanted to pull each and every eyelash out of my brown eyes. What were these two people thinking? The dude was missing digits because of his blood sugar levels, He had thick white cream dangling from his

Brenda Wojick

unkempt salt and pepper beard, and he had the covers pulled down showing his half naked body. I wish there were a nicer word for gross.

"Please, no Boston cream donuts on my time. This is part of the reason you are here." I explained as he was forcing in the donut. I wanted a light from above to shine down on me as I commanded, "Put the donut down, NOW."

"My sugars are in control," he stated and wife interjected "He's doing much better now."

"All due respect to the both of you, he is missing a toe because of his blood sugar. Put the donut down, and you can't have it here while you are in the hospital under our care, my care."

Some people just never learn. Count the toes, 1, 2, 3, 4, 5, 6, 7, 8, 9…..that's it, 9. Nine toes. He has four on one foot and five on the other. The last time I checked we should have five toes on one foot and five toes on the other. When you do the math, 5+5=10. For Ralph, 4+5=9. Simple mathematics people. Put the fucking donut down.

A few hours later his call light went off and I went in..

"I need help," he whined.

"What can I do for you?" I calmly asked.

"I need the urinal."

"Ralph, why can't you do this yourself? You are a young man and you must take care of this on your own at home. What's the deal? We have been down this lovely road before"

96

Can You Squeeze My Banana?

"I'm paralyzed at the hips," he replied. He was not. This was a classic case of sheer L-A-Z-I-N-E-S-S.

"Ralph," I reply, "even if you were paralyzed at the hips, you do not have bilateral splints on your hands, and your fingers work quite well. Earlier, I actually witnessed them putting a donut into your mouth. Here's your urinal I will give you the privacy you need."

Was he for real, I asked myself as I smacked my own forehead. He could use his call bell exceptionally well, why couldn't he place the urinal down below in the Netherlands?

I was in the med room and all I could hear was, "Nurse, nurse, I need help!"

This had to be my patient. Who else in the world could he be screaming for? Ralph was in a panic. I went running into the room .He shouted out to me, "I need a suppository." Well of course he did, this would be his reason for the gut wrenching screams. "I need a suppository! I asked three days ago!" Mind you he hadn't even been here for three days. "Ralph, we would prefer it if you could use your call bell please. A suppository is not an emergency."

"I don't know where the call bell is," he stated.

I was losing my mind at this point. Gone, adios.

"It's on your stomach. It would be great if you could use it." My teeth were going to splinter if I ground them any harder than I already was.

Brenda Wojick

Then Ralph asked me sweetly, "While you are here, could you help me with the urinal?"

Car is out of the garage

"What matters is not the length of the wand, but the magic in the stick"

Anonymous

I once had this particular patient who was a pleasant guy, but shall we say that he was very… meager. One should not judge, but then one might not have a good book. This gentleman was in his sixties, and he

Brenda Wojick

could not take his freakin' finger off of the nurses call bell. For example, he would ring the bell, I would go running like a good little nurse. "Put my oxygen on," he would bellow out.

"It's right there next to you on the bed," I pointed out to him.

"I can't do it," he replied.

I wasn't surprised, but I tried anyway.

"You can put it right back in your nose especially since it fell right out of there, you know it can go back in," I said nicely. About 15 minutes later he rang again. I ran, well, walked briskly, maybe saunter was more like it, to the room. He had his back to me looking out the window. This guy was wearing his own little green and blue plaid pajama bottoms the ones that have the little door in the front so that men can urinate from it because we all know how hard it is to pull down pajama pants to go to the bathroom. He turned around. My god, the car was out of the garage!!! He was backing out and going for a ride straight towards me. Picture this visual: he turned around, hands on his hips facing the door and his penis, yes penis, is peeking out of the hole in the front of his fine plaid pj's. The penis and I made eye contact! Just what I needed. Now I was talking to his penis, not to the hand, not to his face, I was talking to the penis. How could you not, when it's dangling where it shouldn't be, out in the open. I wasn't sure what to do. Do I run and hide? Do I make a mention that Mr. Johnson is taking a wee peek around the room checking out the facility? I know, I can ask him to back that thing

Can You Squeeze My Banana?

up and put him away and let's call it a day. What did I really do, well; I just continued our conversation pretending that his pee pee wasn't really there at all. I attempted to focus all of my attention on looking at the top of his head where his hair was sticking up like a cockatoo (no pun intended) from his bed head. I wish there was a section under the hospital protocol manual like under let's say Section 2, paragraph 6, Peeking Penis and how to flee the scene. End of conversation!

Can't find it

"Hey Brenda, are you busy right now," one of the nurses said as they approached me looking as if something was up. I knew that look, and I knew I should ignore her, roll over and play dead.

"No, what's up," I asked.

"I need help putting a Foley catheter in one of my patients. I have to call down to central supply to see if they have the Foleys that are a bit stiffer than the 16 French that we have on the floor."

Before I even asked why she needed a stiffer Foley, (stiff and Foley should not be in the same sentence) I should have definitely known better. It was one of those crazy days up on 3 and anything was possible at this point.

I said to her, "you have the patient in room 8 don't you?" She could only smile. I knew that the patient in room 8 was a very large gentleman, nah, obese gentleman, no, wait a minute, words cannot describe the size of this person. Looking at my small frame, I weigh roughly 125 lbs. This man was 4 times my weight. This should give you

102

Can You Squeeze My Banana?

a clear picture of the size of the patient I would be dealing with here. His penis was disguised in costume by rolls of skin, therefore making it just about close to impossible not only to find and identify the male genitalia but even more impossible to get a full grip on it just enough to insert a Foley catheter into the penis. Ahhh! These are the days I love my job and I reminisce about the good ole nursing school days and remember the time I said, "I want to be a nurse." These are the days that you must maintain a sense of humor because sometimes you do feel you will fall apart at the seams and will become one very frustrated nurse. Nurse or no nurse, I am a human being, and therefore I still get emotional. I generally handle each day on the calendar including my profession with a giddy sense of humor. This is how I get through most days. I do believe that if you cannot find pleasure in the job that you do every day, definitely discounting the task of touching this dude's rocket, it would most definitely be impossible to come to work on a daily basis. I certainly don't wake up every day hoping to insert a Foley catheter into a large man, or changing and cleaning up after a huge bowel movement explosion, but I choose to smile and laugh inside. Okay, you got me? Some days I have to laugh on the outside too. Not everyone that I know appreciates this quality, but you know what, it doesn't matter.

Patients are people too, and they have feelings, and I would never do anything intentionally to hurt anyone's feelings. That would be entirely unethical. The patient's feelings are put first at all times when

Brenda Wojick

it comes to their care, and I work very hard to help my patient and their needs. Some days you just have to say, "What the F***?" Not out loud of course.

Getting back on track, I was trying to decide how I was going to handle this situation without humiliating my patient, when who did I see but one of the surgeons that was well known to us coming up to the floor and another MD, who both became involved in our conversation. He had just gone in to see the patient that we are discussing and mentioned to me with a sinister snicker that it is days like today he was glad he could ask the nurse to insert the Foley.

This was not my patient. I was just there to help. RNs have got to back up our fellow nurses. We always have each other's back because we would want them to have ours, especially when you are ready to pass out from gross encounters.

I was a newbe nurse (new to the profession) so I was willing to do just about anything to get the experience. I walked into the patient's room to fully assess the situation at hand, and in my head I can only say "holy shit!" Please excuse my language. I didn't say it out loud, only to myself. God bless the inner monologue.

If you are nearly 500 pounds your body can only stretch so far, and your skin has to roll and hang somewhere and being on earth gravity takes over and brings it down. Down where? Well, down over the genitalia in question. On top of saying wholly shit in my head I was also saying, "Oh my god, where do I begin, how do I begin?" Well, I have found in nursing the only way to begin is to go full steam ahead. Jump right in there and get your feet wet. If you assess the situation long enough you will not want to do it, believe me, and you know you have to. I removed the stethoscope from my neck (I didn't want it getting lost), and I removed my scrub jacket that I was wearing because I was now sweating from every inch of my body. It felt like it was 100 degrees in the room. To make it worse, whenever I put rubber gloves on I sweat. I have no idea why, but the rubber on my hands and doing procedures in these tiny little rooms brings the temperature up in my body, oh, about 20 extra degrees.

I put my gloves on my hands. I had two other people with me in the room, the nurse who has this patient and a nursing assistant, and believe you me; we were going to need all the help that we can get. The process here is one that involved pulling up the patient's Johnny, spreading the legs, and putting all of the sterile equipment that we need on the bed as close to the penis as we can to keep the area as sterile as possible because we are inserting a foreign object into the urethra and my job is to minimize the risk of infection (see, I can be serious and knowledgeable). What I had now was a person who had thighs and calves the size of me on each side. Come on, envision this with me, two little people for legs that I had to move. Impossible. It took two of us. I'm a nurse, not a bodybuilder. Now, I had to find the penis. I know

Brenda Wojick

what the penis looks like, I am a nurse, I have a husband, and a son, and this was not the first time I have ever had to perform this procedure, but for some reason I could not identify the penis. I was questioning myself now, am I in the right spot, has it been moved since the last time I've seen one, did it just fall off? I couldn't find it. How do I handle this in a professional way? I asked for assistance and had the other two girls with me attempt to hold up skin and rolls. In my head, once again I am saying to myself, roll, roll, scrotum, and roll. I knew I was close because I saw testicles! Yes! You can imagine my excitement when I discovered this. I composed myself and asked the nursing assistant to hold this up, meaning; you guessed it, his skin. It took two people to handle this task. Then I saw it, the head of the penis! I felt as though I had just won the lottery. Now I planned in my head how I was going to grab the one eyed creature and insert this Foley. At this point I just want to scream, "Can someone wipe the beads of sweat off of my forehead?" I chuckled a bit and just went for it. It was like a jungle struggle. It went to the left, it wiggled to my right, and it even sucked back inward once or twice. The beast was fighting me here, and I wasn't going to lose. It was a slippery little guy that just had to be put down. Unfortunately, much to my surprise, I lost the battle. Oh, I got a handle on the little guy, but I was not successfully able to insert the Foley catheter. For some reason on entry it would recoil inside. It just would not go straight in. I was totally

Can You Squeeze My Banana?

defeated after the fight! I returned from battle with my head hung low, and some laughs at the nurse's station. Better luck next time.

Rated P for Penis

"When you become senile, you won't know it"

Bill Cosby

Since we have been on the subject of the penis, let's continue on with another good ole story perhaps one that you do not want to read to the children for a bedtime story. "Brenda, can you come in here, Mr. Big is going to hurt himself," stated one of the nursing techs. I'm thinking to myself, this guy has on wrist restraints, he is a 1:1 supervision, and what could he possibly be doing in there to harm himself. She's giggling, "Well, he has a hold of himself pretty tight in there." "Himself," I said. That's another reason why I enjoy writing these stories. I can give the male anatomy all sorts of names now can't I?

How the heck do you get an eighty something year old man to let go of his wee wee? It's actually quite simple, you don't.

Mr. Big, is not really with it at this time hence the restraints. He's very restless, and he has a depends on at this time. A depends is a big person's diaper, not quite as cute as your little boys diaper I might add.

Can You Squeeze My Banana?

Anyway, I get into the room, and he somehow has his diaper pulled to the side, his wee wee is out to the side, and he has an absolute killer grip on it, so tight that I can see the tip turning purple.

"Mr. Big, you appear to be hurting yourself." I say. I am trying to remain professional and not laugh. "No," is his response. "You have quite a grip on your penis." (Giggling) I hate using the big boy terms. "No," is his reply once again with the biggest smile spread across his entire face just like a kid who was caught with his hand in the cookie jar. This is getting way too much for me! "Mr. Big, can you put the penis down," as I try to maintain a straight and professional face. "Please let go and put it down," attempting to free willy myself without any success. He was all teeth at this point grinning ear to ear. This, mind you, was the most I've ever heard my patient speak. He never ever speaks. Today the penis police are not on duty at the hospital. Imagine being on that code team. PLAN P PENIS GRIP, PLAN P PENIS GRIP ON 3. "We'll cover him up and look the other way." Call me if it falls off because there is nothing I can possibly do. I can only shake my head. It's a jungle out there!

Balloon Knot

The wonders of the elephant's trunk, the balloon knot, the cowl neck sweater…these are all the nicknames of the infamous uncircumcised penis! In case you didn't know and wanted to find out, many older gentlemen are not circumcised, at least not the male patients that I've encountered.

It was a good day, and I can't really say that too often on our surgical floor. It is getting much tougher to take care of people due to the acuity of the patient's illness these days. I get stressed and out of control as well as many of other nurses that I work with do, but I do get through it and everyone else does too. I was getting ready to discharge my 73 year old male patient who is in room 41A, a nice gentleman. It was sort of an easy discharge I must add, and that's when I realized this is too easy. Well, it didn't surprisingly enough. He was an alert, oriented, pleasant gentleman. He had a procedure that we call "roto rooter" and more specifically that is when a male patient who has issues with his bladder and prostrate undergoes a procedure called a TURP in which

110

essentially he will have tissue removed from his prostate. That is what this gentleman had, and afterwards he had a Foley catheter placed. All I had to do was remove his Foley, and make sure he urinated before being discharged. I did it! Yep, I sure did. I removed his Foley, he had foreskin there which I then rolled down back into place, snug as a bug. He urinated not once, but he urinated twice for me a total of 350 cc's. He stated no blood, no pain just pee Okay, free to go according to the MD's orders. He was a little swollen around his "mushroom cap," but nothing that was out of the ordinary since he did have the big "clean out." Things are great, days go good, and I go home for the night. Whew!

The next morning I came to work just like any other day, and opened and read all of my emails to see everything that is exciting and new. There was an email sent to me by one of the supervisors regarding this man and how he ended up in the emergency room the night before because his foreskin was not folded back down so apparently the rest of his manhood became swollen. He actually came to the emergency room, paid a co-payment for his insurance, sat there most of the night to wait for a nurse to roll down his floppy foreskin. He, or his wife, could have done that free of charge.

I was so flippin' mad as I was reading this email because I felt like they were unleashing the foreskin police on me. He was alert and could fix the malfunction under the hood of his own car. After I had removed

Brenda Wojick

the Foley he urinated twice, it should be his fault for not rolling the cowl neck sweater back in its place. Should I have gone home with him and his wife and followed him in the bathroom each time he urinated to make sure he covers his head with a sweater? I could see if he didn't have use of his hands or fingers, but come on. He could pee; he could roll it back down! I was walking around the nurse's station like a big baby stomping my feet. I'm a nurse, not a babysitter, and certainly not a mechanic. Jeez, and this, come to find out, was his second trip to the emergency room for the same incident. One time is bad enough but two. Has this man not had dangling foreskin his entire life? He must have seen the head of his penis come up for a breath of fresh air and should have realized that his is usually covered, maybe he should fix that.

Rancid Milk

"Does somebody, anybody have something I can ram up my nose? If I roll over and play dead will she walk away?" Those were the thoughts that were running rapidly through my mind as a crazy patient came to the nurse's station by walking over there on her own two feet to tell me that she was dying, needed medical attention, we weren't helping her, and wanted a wheelchair because she was leaving. One word came to my mind, but I'll give you a hint: two syllables, it's a movie, it starred Anthony Perkins, and it rhymes with "Miko."

While I understood that someone who thought they were dying might actually *want* to stay in the hospital, I really wanted nothing more than this particular lady to leave the nurses station. Surprisingly enough, she was not my patient because the crazy ones usually are, but this time I was covering a lunch for a co-worker when this woman decided to start acting ridiculous. I began to pray, *Dear Lord, almighty great one, grand Wizard of Oz, little green leprechaun, anyone??? Please make her go away.* I had to literally sniff the ink off of the paper that I

Brenda Wojick

had in front of me because this woman smelled so bad she could have peeled paint off of the walls. Wow! I looked behind me and expected to see all of the other nurses passed out on the floor or even worse, dead. With the look of sheer horror in their eyes they were behind me sniffing antibacterial hand gel, some ran and a few I think were even crying. I would have preferred sniffing rancid chunky milk that was left out in the sun all day, that's how bad the stench was. *Don't let me pass out, please don't let me pass out* was all that I kept thinking. She had refused to let us wash her from the day she was admitted, and call me nuts, but I'm assuming that at home there are no Calgon moments in her daily regimen.

As we were letting her go against medical advice, or AMA as we like to call it, we had to make sure that her IV was removed. That means that someone, and not me, would have to get close enough to remove the damn thing. The patient stated that she had been a nurse at one point, (poor patients) and that under "antiseptic" technique she had already pulled it out. "Antiseptic" technique, geez that reminds me of mouthwash. Well, whatever, she pulled it out anyway. Okay, please go now!

She called herself a cab as she left the hospital against our medical advice. Poor cabbie. As I got home I turned on the 6:00 news to see if there were any cab drivers that were rushed to the hospital due to asphyxiation. Luckily, there wasn't. Good bye, good riddance!

No Hablo Espanola

In my nursing career, the whole five years of it, I have come across a language barrier situation (or two). Our facility is a hospital outside of Boston, although culturally diverse, we are not as diverse as the larger Boston hospitals Every now and then we get an adorable (I use that word loosely) elderly patient that doesn't speak any English. Up in this neck of the woods it tends to be Spanish or Portuguese, but either way, No Hablo Espanol. I barely speak English most times. It tends to be Slangish with, a hint of Boston accent, so needless to say unless the patient is saying to me "Tengo Una Cita Con Jose" (translated it means, "I have a date with Jose") I haven't the slightest idea what is being said to me. They can swing their arms, get closer even talk loud, and I still don't get it. Just like when I attempt to speak to them HOW – ARE- YOU – FEELING? Loud and annoying and I'm not understood either.,.

We had a non English speaking Hispanic male, on our floor, who to had dementia to boot.. He wouldn't lie in bed, he wouldn't sit in the chair, by the time we reached the bed alarm, he was already making his rounds attempting to visit other patients in their rooms. The nursing assistants would sit with him and walk him around the hallways, and everybody who worked on our floor attempted their version of speaking Spanglish to him which was quite a comical relief in itself. IT WAS JUST TOO MUCH. There was no way possible to explain to him for his safety he needed to stay put. "El Pute." Duct tape entered my mind at one point, but I would then find myself on the 6:00 news for sure.

Lois, another RN and one of my awesome friends, had been working all day with me, and she had been trying to entertain this patient. She would just grab onto his hand, and she would do a little two step slow dance. We are not talking lap dances here people, we are talking a foot and a half space between them, with the patient holding onto her hand and they would just twirl in a circle. He would smile, calm down and we would keep him quite for a little while longer. Still no hablo English though. This worked for a couple of days and it would quiet this gentleman down. Lois and the rest of us could go on with our business.

The next day I was having a conversation with one of the doctors about a patient of mine when this other little guy started it up again. He was getting up and trying to walk around to other people's rooms, when Lois stepped up to the plate to help us out! She started the dancing routine. They were in the hallway near the nurse's station. It was safe, we can all see them, and he was smiling having a grand ole time when

116

Can You Squeeze My Banana?

his little hand decides that it wants to mosey on down to Lois' behind area, not quite touching the buttocks, but you can tell he would have loved to. In the blink of an eye, boom…..he goes full throttle and thrusts his entire pelvic area into her leg, just once! And once was all it took! Humping has no language barriers, it is a universal language. He had a devious smile on his face, and we were stunned. Well, we were sort of stunned. I am at that point where almost nothing is surprising anymore. Of course we laughed about this, hysterically I might add. What else could we do, break his hands? We now waited for him to speak fluent English and ask her out on a date. I wouldn't put anything past this character. Somehow I think he knew how to speak English, and he knew exactly what he was doing.

Psych floor

Are you kiddin' me? Some of the nurses may say that it's the luck of the draw; others may verify it is who does the schedule for the day. You can always sense how your day is going to go when you walk down the hallway in the morning at 7:00 am. On this day I was getting bad vibes. Oh, the guy at the end of the hall was moaning louder than a dog in heat. As I made my way down the hall I could hear aaaahhhhhhh, aaahhhh. Mmmmaaawww. This began on Saturday morning; I worked all weekend and Monday into Monday evening. He never stopped once. Not once.

My patient load for the next three days included a middle aged gentleman who was detoxing from alcohol, a psychotic female who has absolutely no reason to be at the hospital, oh yeah, a man who goes by the name Jesus, as in the big kahuna from above. I guess the acute care setting has been put on hold and this weekend we are officially a psych ward. If I were to work in a psych ward at least I could medicate them and let them be, but not here. We have to actually deal with them for hours on end. Deep breath…..

One of my patient's this particular weekend was a lady who was classified as a 1:1, where a tech sat with her so that she didn't hurt herself. She was missing her front tooth and demanding to see her doctor. She was a homeless female who was medically fine, but mentally burnt out. The hospital offered to put her up in a hotel for the weekend, she refused. They offered to send a cab and pick her up and take her to a shelter, but she told me, "I would rather live under a tree."

"That's your choice," I told her. I called the psychiatrist to the floor, only to have her tell the doctor and myself that this patient was well known to our psyche floor, and she was banned from there. Banned, are you friggin kidding me, banned from a psyche floor?? How bad is she that she is no longer allowed on the floor where she should be? She can't even mingle with the insane people, that's how crazy she is. How was I going to care for her? Very carefully.

My other patient was showing positive signs for withdrawing from his vodka binge. I walked into his room and from the fumes on his breath I believe I became totally inebriated. All of a sudden I was dizzy. His pores were oozing alcohol. Anybody's eyes would have burned if they entered his room. Nice dude, many problems, and he's all mine to take care of. From afar I can hear Chewbacca from *Star Wars* moaning and carrying on in his room with that relentless never ending chant

Brenda Wojick

Then we eventually got Jesus. Jesus, as I was taught, walked on water, not in the halls of our hospital spitting mucus, screaming for his lawyer and continuously begging for a cigarette. He was completely schizophrenic! He was supposed to be confined to his room but he would not stay put. He was confrontational, and although he called himself "Jesus," he hates nuns. He asks every female that approaches his room "Are you a F*&%ing nun?" Even if you were, would you admit it at this point in time? Although, I would have loved to introduce him to Sister Satan at this point in time.

Crazy lady was ranting in the hallways looking for me, making the craziest of patients look normal. She was short with long scraggly gray hair, stereotypical, but you know the kind. Women at that age should never be allowed to have long hair -especially if they have "crazy" people issues. She was now demanding to see the Chaplin, a Rabbi, the doctor, the nurse, anybody. She was removing her clothing in front of the tech, stating, "I never used to look like this. I used to be pretty." Her sagging boobs and tummy were just hanging in front of her. "My god please put some clothes on. You can't walk around like this," I begged.

We had everyone we need on the floor: the clinical coordinator, me, other nurses and security. Security was a key factor here since we were escorting her off of the hospital grounds. We had arranged to have her taken by cab into Boston to one of the homeless shelters. The cab would be taken care of by the hospital, and the driver was given

Can You Squeeze My Banana?

specific instructions on where to drive her. About 6 nurses and other nursing assistants were all in one room, watching her being escorted off of the property and put into the cab. It is almost comical because she gets in the cab and the cab just sits there. It doesn't leave. The cab was out by the valet section of the hospital, and security had already walked back into the hospital. The cab just sat, and waited, and sat some more. Finally security came back out and told him that he had to go. Well, once a con artist always a con artist. She was gone now, or so we thought.

The hospital received a call from the patient's Rabbi with the exciting news that she ended up having the cab driver take her north instead of south and she wound up at her Rabbi's house. He was calling us wondering what he should do with her. Are you kidding me, we just got rid of her, she's in your house now buddy.

Addicted

Burned booby flesh, now that's a wake up aroma that I had never smelled until today. I bet you are wondering how a quadriplegic burns her boob. Actually, I was wondering. I first became privy to this information when I found out that this female, 50 or so years of age, would be one of my five patients. She had a bowel movement, to say the least, but the tech did not want to change her because she had two burn spots right above the nipple line on her left breast. It would have been a major assumption on my part about how she actually came to have a burn there, but she had two very deep craters on her flesh as if she picked, picked and picked again at this nipple skin. Now it was actually oozing, and knowing that this odd little patient is a quad, I wondered how the heck this happen. Did I dare ask how this happened considering she has almost no use of her hands?

I walked into the room which smelled like an ashtray, and saw the patient laying flat in her hospital bed in a soiled Johnny with her left boob completely exposed. Her sister, who was her caretaker at

122

Can You Squeeze My Banana?

home, was keeping her company in the room. They were both obviously smokers because the room smelled enough to make even the Marlboro man sick if he wasn't already dead from lung cancer. On her boob were two dime size lesions that were now oozing pus and blood, and thank god I haven't had my morning coffee yet. This lady could barely move her hands and arms. She was completely flaccid and she was a smoker. That's a tough vice to have when you can't reach your mouth. When I came in and asked the patient how she received these wounds, the sister stated, "She's a smoker. I try time and time again to get her to quit she just won't."

Now let's think this through. Having already established that the patient has no use of her arms, I was now trying to figure out how the hell she got a cigarette to her mouth from the limp position she was in. Apparently, the cigarette must have fallen from her mouth onto her boob and burnt it. She could have taken the nipple right off. From the look of the depth of the wound, that cigarette sat there for a couple of seconds in order to burn through the flesh, or so I thought. I would have enjoyed saying to the sister, "Getting her to quit seems to be an open and shut case to me. If she isn't moving her arms, there's no way for her to bring that butt up to her mouth no matter how much she wants it unless you bring it to her."

Not only did the sister ,bring the ciggie butt up to her mouth to suck on the damn thing, but while her boob was oozing pus in the

123

Brenda Wojick

hospital, her kind sister decided to pop the blister for her as if it were a pimple. She actually grabbed the boob and squeezed at the nipple until it exploded. How gross. Now how's that for helping out your sibling? "Honey, remember when you dropped the cigarette on me, could you now start picking at my nipple line until it becomes the biggest crater and then let's watch it bleed. You're the best." Clearly smoking cessation is not going to help here because as long as the sister gets them and jams them into her mouth, the patient will smoke and her boob will ooze pus.

Flying objects

"When you've seen a nude infant doing a backward
somersault you know why clothing exists"
Stephen Fry

I came out of my patient's room in 12 at 8:00 in the morning and grabbed Catherine, who was the nurse's assistant assigned to work with me today. "I have to go to the ER, I think I broke my baby toe," I said to her frantically. I was certain Catherine was not going to believe my story.

I had to assist one of the MD's in the room with rolling a patient over onto her side because she had Multiple Sclerosis and was bed ridden, so away I went. I went in, rolled the patient away from me towards the wall so that her backside was facing me and it was like a cannon shot off. It shot something straight at me, and it was hard as a rock. Oh, God I did know what it was, and I didn't even want to look. I wish I could have held my breath and eventually passed out to make this moment disappear. I heard, tink, and then felt something hit the

Brenda Wojick

tip of my white nursing shoe. Don't look down, don't look down, I kept saying to myself, girl, you know what it is, don't even go there! I looked! Peeked first with one eye looked hard next. A giant ca-ca ball the size of a golf ball was rolling in slow motion right under her bed. The ca-ca ball was a fine start to my day because it could not get any better with her or any other patient. Ahh, decisions and dilemmas. Do I pick up the ca-ca ball, or do I leave the ca-ca ball? What would you do? Do I pretend that it never hit me and go on my zingy way, as I tactfully look over my shoulder to see if there are any eye witnesses to the hoopla? Should I page housekeeping – we have the removal of a ginormous ca-ca ball under the bed, would you mind removing that? What the hell is she going to do with that, what the hell am I going to do with that? It's not something I feel comfortable picking up. With all my bad BM luck I should be carrying around a personal pooper scooper. Slide it under the bed, plop, and away I go. I feel like picking it up and giving it back to the patient and asking her to hold onto it since she's the person who dropped it. Should I mark this on her belonging sheet from when she first came into the hospital and attach it to the list of things she brought it with her? But no, I gloved up and got ready for combat. I got to my knees and down to my elbows, swiped it up and disposed of it properly by putting it in her pocketbook (nah, just kidding), then I began to sanitize the heck out of my shoe. Of course, I had to go tell my story.

Meanwhile, the gentleman in the room next to her was very unhappy, in fact, so unhappy that the whole hallway heard that he was upset about the French toast that he was attempting to have for breakfast. You see, the kitchen made a silly little mistake of cutting it in half, and this just threw him right over the edge and into a frenzy. He was loud, he was boisterous and there was no comforting this man, no, no, no. The kitchen messed with his French toast, and guess what he used to do for a living- he used to be a cook, so apparently he knows better. I should have known better and just stayed away, but being his nurse, this would be difficult, and besides he was like a hall monitor standing in his doorway all day just yelling, and yelling and yelling.

He called me over and asked me, "What is this?" He was holding something shiny in his hand.

"It's a spoon," I replied.

"It's not the right one. You can't eat anything with this, and I know my spoons." I am daring, and I enjoy living life on the edge, so I asked, "What can't you eat with that spoon?"

"Look at this," he said as he was splashing in cream of wheat, "Look at it." I was staring and truly I was concentrating, but what was I missing?

"I can't eat this; it looks like a bird shit three times in here."

That just gave me a whole new look on cream of wheat, which I decided I would never eat again and yes, thank you for the image that

Brenda Wojick

will forever be etched in my mind. I took his tray away and attempted to order him another one, but not before he stole the silverware from the tray. Apparently, this had been his new found hobby during his hospitalization because I found silverware in the drawers next to him and in his bed under the covers. I wasn't quite sure what that was all about, I didn't really want to know. I just wanted him to give me the darn silverware back. Well, for three more precious hours he yelled, ranted and raved about the cut in half French toast. Even the crazy patients on the floor were saying he was crazy. Hah.

The lady in the other room was making fun of me. It was great. She hated my hair, told me I look like Cher and then called me conceited. She didn't want me touching her because of my hair. What the hell gives?

Remember the dude that always wanted the urinal but had nothing wrong with his hands and loved his Boston Cream donuts? He had come back for another guest appearance on 3, continuing on the noncompliant diabetic path. He was persevering on the downhill slope to non-recovery. He was already minus his big toe on the right foot, and he just might be losing another little piggy to the butcher market. He was not to ambulate or put any weight on that foot while he was on our floor. My job was to be an over qualified babysitter for the time that he was here. Simple request: stay in bed, foot elevated. His bed alarm was ringing constantly because he just had to do exactly what he

Can You Squeeze My Banana?

was told not to do. He was so unsteady on his feet it was ridiculous. He happened to also be a young man, as previously mentioned so he should be able to listen. He asked for his pain medication and I sprinted down the hallway, leaping hurdles to get it immediately, figuring it just might make him fall asleep. I was guessing he was going to be hitting the call bell every five minutes instead.

"Can I get up?" he asked.

"No, you cannot."

"Can I get up and walk?"

"NO." This went on for an hour. When he rang again, I went into the room. He was figuring that if he worded the question in a different way, I might give him a different answer.

"Brenda, can you ambulate me?"

"Can you get some toes first and then we'll go walking!"

At this point, I think the clump that I was feeling in my hand was the hair from my head after I had pulled it out. It was only 9:30 in the morning, and I was scared, because it wasn't going to get any better than this.

Never Underestimate

I had heard about this young man from the previous shifts, and I had seen him ambulating in the hallway and standing at his doorway, which is by the nurse's station. He always had this very blank stare on his face. I knew I was in for more than I'd bargained for.

He was a 33 year old male patient who came to us a few days before with change in mental status. These are always oldies but goodies because everyone digs in the trenches to find the reason for this confusion. This dude did have some mild mental retardation, but his family had stated that he's been acting "weird" and he'd been making strange gestures and remarks. They knew that something just wasn't right, so they brought him into our ER where he was then admitted to our floor. I had not had the pleasure of caring for him until one Monday in July. That was my first and very only day that I was ever going to be his nurse. I also had a student extern orienting with me at this time. We were in report listening to the tape of the previous nurse. She stated that there was some inappropriate behavior by this patient on the evening

130

shift the day before. At this point I'm thinking, *why me?* I suppose *why not?* Apparently, he had touched the evening nurse's bum bum when she turned to walk away. He was also making some unfitting hand movements down by his, shall I say, pee pee area. I laughed it off and didn't give it a second thought. Stupid stuff like this has happened before.

I went in first thing in the morning and introduced myself to this young man. I explained to him that I would be his nurse for the day. Both of his parents were present and were also quite concerned about his situation so they had roomed in with the patient all night. The young man was very cooperative, and he answered all of my questions appropriately. It just appeared that he really wanted to go home, but before anyone was to discharge him, he need to be seen by the neurologist and have a lumbar puncture performed by him at the bedside. The patient was just taking it in stride, and every now and then asking if he could go home after the procedure.

12:30 p.m. came and the doctor had arrived on the floor. I asked if the student nurse could be present with us during the lumbar puncture. This isn't the easiest thing to go through when you are all alone. A needle is placed in between your vertebrae while fluid is drained from the space in between. The patient must lie perfectly still in a fetal like positioned curled up in a ball. I truly felt bad for the patient, especially since he had some mental delay. I didn't know if he quite understood

Brenda Wojick

what was about to happen or the severity of it all. I guess at that time I didn't realize what was about to happen to me during the lumbar puncture.

I was standing close to the wall on the inside of the room, the doctor was closer to the door while the student nurse was standing with her back up against the window watching the whole procedure. I was trying to be a good little nurse and stand in front of the patient to offer him some emotional support. Much to my surprise he had something else in mind at this time. I think he thought it was our first date. He had asked me if I could hold his hand while this took place. He looked scared. I felt so bad, and had no problem with holding his hand, that is what I am there for. I do this for many of patients. He had his hands on top of my hands which are on top of the bed, and separating the two of us is the bedrail. His body is pushed way over on the other side of the bed for this procedure and it is as if he has to reach to get my hands. I was watching very closely when I felt his right hand move ever so slightly away from my left hand. It moved towards my wrist. Not worried, not yet anyway! I was concentrating on what the doc was doing to his back. It was very fascinating. Then his hand came up to the side of the bedrail that was in between us to take a rest just before the violation occurred. Ever so slyly and nonchalantly, he stuck out his index finger as his hand made its way towards my boob. I grabbed his hand and moved it back towards the bed hoping that this is all just a big misunderstanding. But

Can You Squeeze My Banana?

there was misunderstanding here, because as soon as I put his hand back, quicker than a dog in heat, he made his second attempt. I looked up over at Darlene with a look of horror on my face. Alrighty then! I told the doctor that the patient was getting a bit frisky with me. Speed it up man. I can't take this. Oh my god, no he didn't. Well, apparently boobies weren't the only thing on his mind, because he took his hand (which I had let go of at this point) and moved it away I was totally creeped out. And then things got creepier. He was jumping jack flash and ever so insidiously pulled down his pants and placed his hand on his little boy. I shot a look over at Darlene and then to the doctor. Oh no, he's going to find another toy to play with because his is not playing with that one while I am in this room with him. I let the doctor know what the hell was transpiring on the other side of the bed, and I asked him to move his hand back for me. This was beyond weird. We moved his hand, and then he wanted me to hold it (his hand) for him, but I was all set with that. All I was thinking was, *"You can go through the rest of this on your own my friend."*

"My penis is sticking out," he begins to tell me. Great. Well, I wasn't putting it back for him. That most definitely was not in my definition of registered nurse.

"Are you married," he asked me. At the time I was not but, "Yes," was my immediate answer, and I can picture Fred just laughing at me. The doctor was at this point attempting to make small conversation

Brenda Wojick

with the patient. *Let's get the hell out of here* is what I am thinking. I'm all set.

I said to the doctor, "I think this means that he and I are dating." I had to tell Lois. "Lois, you are never going to believe this shit"! My guy in 12, he is the most knowledgeable confused guy I have ever seen. Yeah, he went for the nipple."

"What," is exactly what Lois said.

" Yep, nipple man tried to grope me while having a lumbar puncture done. Can you believe this crazy crap?" I leaned over to the doctor to yell over my shoulder, "Are you going to be the ring bearer at the wedding?"

He replied, "That was the most porn I have ever seen here."

Each day we write a nursing note on our patients. It is an update for the next shift and other medical personnel to look at and get the idea of what is going on with the patient. Naturally, it has to be well written and in a professional manner. I wish I could type exactly what happened and with my words. It would go a little something like this....

Patient alert, oriented, apparently not confused at all. His vital signs are stable, afebrile, lung sounds are clear. Patient did have a bedside lumbar puncture performed by the neurologist. Patient whipped out his pee pee and attempted to slap it on me while bustin' a move on me trying to fondle my nipples in front of on lookers. Patient does not appear confused at all, and he knows right where his penis lies. He knows where a female's breasts' sit and

Can You Squeeze My Banana?

he also has some bad lines to work with. Patient will be ready for discharge as soon as we can pry his hand from his pants.

Colonoscopy

"When humor goes, there goes civilization"
Erma Bombeck

If you can't laugh at yourself who the hell can you laugh at? I've shared many stories with you about people that I have come in contact with over the years and the situations that have made me shake my head and roll my eyes, but in this story the tables have turned, and I am the patient.

So the joke was on me because I found out from my doctor that I was going to be the victim of a colonoscopy...or two. Each and every day, it never fails just when I have to go to the bathroom; I get paged to the nurse's station. It irritates the daylights out of me. I swear there are candid cameras hanging around ready and waiting to piss me off, so needless to say it is a whole process to go to the biffy. First, I have the mental preparation which is everything. Nurses tend to hold all bodily waste in all day because they do not have any time to go to the bathroom. Once I get over the mental preparation, timing is paramount because I actually have to fit this into my schedule. Do I go before I give medications, after medications, before I document, when my patient falls asleep…you get the point. Then I totally worry, will I have enough time when I get in there before I get the page. I am totally stressed out about the mere act of going to the bathroom. I'm sure Mother Nature didn't intend for it to be this way. Who has ever heard of such a ridiculous thing? I think I need an Ativan to talk myself down; it's only the bathroom Brenda. Pick a time and go!

Now that I've decided I am actually going to go to the bathroom, I actually have the decision to make on which friggin' bathroom to use. The staff bathroom is very tiny and stuffy. This is designated for peeing purposes only! No Pooping in there. It's too small. We use the public bathroom down the end of the hallway which is much larger than the staff bathroom. This one is designated the BM bathroom. This is where the poopie happens. Whatever happens at the end of the hall stays at the end of the hall. At this point I decide to go in and assess my patient with Darlene, student extern, when my gastrointestinal tract decided to speak louder than my patient. You know that god awful grumbling rumbling massive eruption noise that comes from deep within, and that's when Darlene and my patient became very silent, and all you could hear was my stomach preparing the toxins for the biggest poop ever and moving ever so slowly down my intestine into the colon area. Mortified, because it so does not sound like hunger pangs, I hope this does not happen

Brenda Wojick

again. Oh yeah baby, it happens again. This is me we are talking about. Darlene laughed and I decided, time to go to the bathroom.

So I make my way down to the "big bathroom" at the end of the hallway, bear with me folks. Untie the scrub pants, waiting for the page, begin to do the whole squat thing that woman do in public bathrooms, turtle head making its way out, and here we go, free and clear. And then, like a voice from above: "Brenda to the nurse's station, Brenda to the nurse's station." Hell, no. I must have looked like a deer in the headlights.

I've had to walk out to the nurse's station leaving unfinished business so often that I now have to see a GI doctor for my "issues." Guess what? Its colonoscopy time and it sounds like one hell of a shindig. I picked a GI doc from the hospital I work at because I trust some of the docs that I've had to deal with, and I've spoken to patients about their experiences. I now have to drink the bowel prep for the next day. I was totally sympathizing with my patients now.

The big day came and my mom took me to the hospital for my appointment. All I could think about as I was going up the highway was that in a very short time, one of the doctors that I work with will see my ass exposed and sticking up in the air while he rams a scope into me. EEEwwww. As I was sitting on a stretcher in the holding area, in my Johnny, naturally trying to look sexy some of the nurses that I know were walking by me. "What are you doing here," one of them asked. *Well, I'm here for some drinks, sandwiches, sodomy with a scope and that would be the end to a mighty fine day.* Dah, hello. "I'm here for a colonoscopy." As soon as I said it, they were wheeling me into the procedure room and getting ready to give me "THE GOOD STUFF." I am referring to the wonderful world of Fentanyl and Versed, both heavy duty medications that provide me with conscious sedation so that I will be sleepy during the procedure. You can still talk, but you don't remember a friggin' word that you've uttered. This was good, because I really do not want to remember the moment that I was curled into a fetal position sucking on my knees with my cellulite ass hanging over the side.

Yep, I was slurring my words right about now, and I remembered asking the nurses not to hold anything I said against me. I was certain that I was sounding positively ridiculous, and I remembered a sharp pain like a knife being raked across my abdomen. Ouch! One of the nurses told me later, "Brenda, you were yelling out, trying to take out your IV, moaning in pain."

"Well, I must have sounded like an idiot," I responded. You can imagine my drugged out state of mind.

The doctor that preformed the colonoscopy came out to talk to me. "Brenda, you will have to come back tomorrow to have it done again." Round two, are you kidding me? Nobody likes having a camera up their butt a first time, never mind twice. This meant no eating or drinking

Brenda Wojick

for another 24 hours. I never really expected my ass to cooperate with me anyhow.

Tomorrow's another day, and don't kid yourself, it comes pretty damn fast when you dread doing something. I made it to the hospital for round number two. I bet you can sense what my excitement levels were at this point. Completely cranky and humiliated I made my way into the procedure room yet once again. Today they were giving me something just a little bit better than the day before, Propofol. It knocks you nearly unconscious. It made headlines as the drug that killed Michael Jackson. Just the way I like it, flat on my back, half dead and in the fetal position sucking my thumb with my ass hairs flapping in the wind. This gives you a true visual of the whole colonoscopy. I promised myself I would be more sympathetic to my patients who have to go through this. Even as they were trying to put the oxygen mask on me I was still trying to talk and crack jokes. Then boom, I was out like a light.

I came to after the procedure feeling like I just got hit by a Mack truck and I have little cotton booties all over my teeth. My lips were stuck to my teeth and barely form any words at this point. "Har die do," I said as I tried to pry my freakin' lips off of my teeth, smacking my tongue across them so that I could sound slightly intelligible, but that didn't work because it felt as if I was smacking a wool blanket across my mouth. Anyway, I made it out fine.

Can You Squeeze My Banana?

The rest of the story was history because all the tests came back normal, but there was just one more deplorable situation yet to go. Now I had to get dressed so that I could leave the hospital. I was looking for my socks which I went into the procedure with on because once my feet are cold, I'm all done. So as I was looking around the nurse came over and handed me a STAT red lab bag with something white in it "When the doctor was doing the procedure, he took out the scope (out of my ass of course) and it snapped back and hit your foot, so we had to remove your socks," she said Oh my head! There was a shit sample on my sock, and then they had been neatly wrapped up, put in a baggie and handed to me. "Okaaaaay, you can fro vem out now," I managed to articulate. My hand was flopping on the bed making every bad attempt to point at the bag. "Aaahhhhcccctttt, gef wid of em, I don't neeeeev em." I felt completely pathetic at this loathsome time in my day, week, and month….life. Can I also just open wide up to you at this time and fill you in on a secret? When they do a colonoscopy, they inject air into your belly so that they can see everything they need to. Guess what you have to do the second you wake up from your procedure? I'm sure you've guessed it, FART. The big F word. It is worse than the other F word at this point in time. You can't ever imagine the amount of air that is expelled from your butt after this is done. Not only do you feel violated (haha) but now you have to embarrass yourself that much more by ripping air like there's no tomorrow. Mommy, time to go home.

Get Off of Him, Not With Him

Last time I looked, we were not running a brothel, or so I thought. As the events continued to take place, however, I began to wonder. The young patients are the absolute worst offenders when they come into the hospital. Unfortunately, they become the neediest and most time consuming of all. I will never understand this. They tend to be the ones who are addicts and are detoxing, and due to their detox they become very ill, but that was not the case with 25 year old Dapper Dan. He was admitted with Crohn's Disease, which affects your bowel and colon. The patient will have massive amounts of diarrhea, cramping and pain. Dan was evidently having a flare up, and undoubtedly needed some attentiveness and hand holding, which as you will see was more than provided for him.

I was charge nurse on this particular day in July. One of my coworkers had Dan in room 29, and she came up to me at one point that morning completely beside herself. Hand up in the air, she cried, "I'm not going back in there, I mean c'mon!"

Can You Squeeze My Banana?

She just could not believe what she was seeing, and I knew that any minute I would feel the same way too and most likely have my hands up in the air. She had brought to my attention that her patient and his chick were curled up in bed together. Here we go again, what are these people thinking! I'm pretty sure I said that out loud. There were other comments were made, but that's probably the cleanest one I made. So, as charge nurse, I became the chosen one, and volunteered to go in.

The zoo that I walked into had spiked hair Mohawk style, facial piercing, and tattoos. These did not bother me; it was the two young individuals intertwined together to the point so you could not tell where one patient ended and where one began, or who the actual patient was for that matter.

"Hello, hello, hi…I'm Brenda; I'm one of the charge nurses here." They didn't respond, possibly because his tongue was lodged down her throat. I continued, "I'm just going to turn off your IV, and I have to ask that you," referring to his girlfriend, "if you please wouldn't mind getting out of the bed." This is really not an odd request to make for someone in the hospital, different story if you're 'pimpin' da hoes', but in this instance he was not. "I haven't seen her in two days," was his response. I wanted to say, "Hey Einstein, who gives a rat's ass," but thankfully I responded much more professionally. "Well, I'm sorry there, but the bed is made for one and one person only." I did have my number one finger up, and no, it was not my middle finger. I'm sure

Brenda Wojick

they could see this, but for good effects, I went with raising the finger anyway. It makes a harsh gesture like; *I am the ruler of this kingdom.* I was thinking to myself, *Just get the hell out of the bed.* "It's really inappropriate to have her in the bed with you," I said, clearing my throat, "and on top of you. We are running a hospital here and you have really sick people around you."

"We shut the door," he said.

Oh my god. Did this kid not get it?

"This isn't a hotel that you are in right now, it's a hospital, the beds are made for one person, and one person only. She has to get out of that bed." I felt like telling him, *don't you get it? My mother, back in the day, would have cuffed me off the top of my head if I was in bed with anyone let alone cuddling in a hospital room.* Besides, let's look at the obvious here, he was sick, he had explosive, nasty diarrhea. Between you and me and everyone who is reading this, I don't see anything remotely romantic about this situation. I walked away hoping I'd made myself clear as to the rules we like to live by here at the hospital.

But apparently they hadn't gotten the message. About an hour later, one of the other nurses came to me in the med room. She's a very nice proper lady, not a bad bone in her body. "I can't go in there again. She's…she's straddling him," she said, horrified. "What," I said. "Oh hell no!" They needed to get over themselves and stop humping on my time. Gross. It's just common sense here. The nurse told me that she was on top of him in the room. Apparently, they both misunderstood the sign on the door at the front entrance. There is no sitting on top of anyone here. We recently installed the NESN channel here because a lot of the men were complaining that is always sports season whether you are sick or not. I didn't realize they installed a porn channel as well!

This time Kim came with me. I thought I was going to explode if I saw her sitting on him, but she was now in front of him leaning on his legs. I was hoping that I was going to handle this in the most profession way that I knew how, but I was just done with the whole situation. I page the physician to explain about sexapades 2007 going on in 29, and the patient needed to get a discharge out of here. It was like a porn show. They could go home and have all the sex they wanted, but not on my time. They were no Pamela Anderson and Tommy Lee, in case you were wondering.

NOTE TO BE POSTED ON THE WALL

There will be no cuddling, kissing, humping, fornicating, touching, feeling up or licking the patient. Nurses do take notice!

My Baby's Daddy

Never go to a doctor whose office plants have died.

-- Erma Bombeck

Now, just down the hallway in the room we like to call the "suite" because it is one of the biggest rooms on the floor, it has a couch, a dresser drawer in it a shower, and a nice TV. We have, well I will have, a young male patient admitted with an irretractable migraine headache, ruled out aneurysm. This is pretty serious stuff for those who have ever heard of an aneurysm but the patient does not appear to think so and neither does his girlfriend. I walk down to the patient's room and there are two people in the bed, familiar scenario! Can't tell which person is the patient, the only dead give-a-way is the name. So I take it the male in the bed is the patient after taking a peek at my assignment sheet, but the female happens to wear the pants in the family. Oh, hell yeah! She defines that statement in every sense of the word. She rolls over and she is about 7 months very pregnant. As nicely as I could I ask her to please get out of the bed. Maybe I rolled my eyes, maybe I didn't, either way,

Can You Squeeze My Banana?

get out of the bed. I need to do a full assessment on what looks like to be "her man." I ask, "Who might this be?" "She's my girl," he says. By the looks of the size of her belly, I was not thinking it was his mother nor his sister, but what I was trying to get at was whether it was his wife, girlfriend or baby's mutha. Either way, get the hell out of the bed. The bed is what got her the big belly in front of her. With a smack of the lips, "just do yo thing why I'm in da bed, I'm tird." This is what she says to me. Do yo thing; I'm thinking saying to myself. What the frig does that mean. If I sighed any louder I would have woken up the guy down the hallway. "Excuse me, hi, trying to capture her attention, but this is a hospital, and we cannot allow two people in a bed here. (Here we go again) I'm sorry, but those are the rules believe it or not," I nicely said this from across the room of course. "Don't be gittin' all up in here." Those are her lips that would be smackin' against one another. Gittin' what the hell is gittin? There must be some bloopers cameras around here somewhere because this is insane. I think that I need to bring an Ebonics translator up in here because this is going to be a difficult day!

The patient is fully dressed at this time and telling, T-E-L-L-I-N-G me that he is just going to go outside for a while. "You can't just go outside. This is not a hotel, you are in the hospital, and you don't get to just go outside. Once you are a patient you are here until we figure out what is wrong with you." "So whatchu be sayin he can't be goin'

147

Brenda Wojick

out?" His girl pipes up. "That is exactly what I am saying. I know that you smoke and you can't go off of the premises to smoke." Yeah, he was gonna do what he was gonna do anyway, so I spoke to the physician and got him a "garden pass" which ultimately meant that he was going to go off the premises to smoke. I just don't understand some people's way of thinking. You were sick enough to bring your ass to the emergency room, so you obvious felt that something was wrong or you wouldn't be here. Just deal with it. When he came back I nicely explained to him that the neurologist wanted to speak with him, so don't go far.

The neurologist came in to see the patient and was out of that room quicker than a cat after a mouse. Before the doctor left I asked him what he thought in regards to questioning an aneurysm. The doctor turned around and appeared as if he was totally annoyed by all means and said he really couldn't get much from the patient because he his "girl" was in the background, they were both on their cell phones, and she seemed to be talking for the patient waving, flailing her arms and speaking for him. That was it! You can tell he was totally put off by this situation. Who wasn't? One of the CA's came up to me to tell me that the female in his room, "the girl," not "the patient," was holding her belly and said to her, "get me sum water, and she was holding onto the pitcher, because my baby get thirsty." "Are you kidding me, she is not even the patient. Gurl, don't let her suck you in. Come get me if you need some help and I will call in my posse if we need them. We

148

laughed; you just had to laugh because this was just so ridiculous." If she was a little more pleasant and a little less ghetto it would make all the difference in the world. You know what else would help, if she would stop flapping those lips at me.

After a whole day of the patient never being in his room, off the floor smoking, filling water pitchers, waiting on them hand and foot, she wanted her "man" to go home. "Well, he can't go home now; he has an MRI that will be scheduled for tomorrow." "Why tomorrow, make it now." She said. I wanted to say that I am not the MRI fairy. I cannot just open my magical appointment book and get one with the snap of a finger. "Their first appointment is tomorrow morning." "We're just gonna leave then." Wanting to let them go, I smiled as best as I could, "You really shouldn't. His situation is serious and an MRI is needed to determine what in fact is going on to cause these headaches." "If it's so serious make his appointment now." She yells to me. "It's serious, but not life threatening at this time, therefore the appointment for tomorrow will suffice." "You be contradickin' yo self be tellin' me it be serious but then not doin' it now. If it so serious git the test done now." This is what she says to me. I want to giggle, but don't want to get bitch slapped in the meantime. "I am not C-O-N-T-R-A-D-I-C-T-I-N-G myself, the situation is serious, and not life threatening at this point, so the first available appointment is given to him. He should stay here incase anything were to happen, he can be monitored. Do realize how

Brenda Wojick

serious this is exactly?" "Do you know I need him at home, he needs to be doin' stuff at home. I'm tird, I'm goin' home." Is what she says. "With all do respect, you are not the patient, so YOU can leave at any time to go home. We are not keeping YOU here, but if he agrees we would like to keep him here, and by the way, I would like to talk to him. Does he ever talk? I don't think this guy talks for himself at all. He is a little puppet on strings being controlled by his girl. Now my arms are flappin' all up in here, I was flustered, and I may have spit a little while I was talking. He, pointing to the dude in the bed, is the patient, and I'm sure he can make this decision by himself. I felt like I needed to put a grill in my mouth with some bling just to get through to them. Shit! "I'm outta here," she said. "That's fine, but he should stay," I nicely said back to her. I walked out of the room and listened by the door as I was working on his flow sheet. "Shit, she be all contradickin herself you dying' but you can't have the test now, you be waitin' till tomorrow. Shit, I'm goin' home. You come home when you be done. You don't be needing no MRI. What she talkin' bout." Yeah, this is what I am hearing. As a nurse, I can only advocate to a certain degree then it becomes a lost situation. Whatever, I still get to go home that day.

I came in the next day and the day after that and I was not as lucky to have him today, but from what I have been told, he was outside with someone drinking. Yes, drinking alcoholic beverages shall we say? And, he had another female in his room, a white one at that, snuggling with

150

Can You Squeeze My Banana?

him the next day. Apparently, we have turned room 1 into a brothel at the end of the hallway, although it is the best room we have to offer! Who really does he think that he is drinking and bringing women into his hospital room whenever he feels like it? For got sakes, have some dignity and enough intelligence to realize that this is ridickalis!!!

Modeling at its finest

Never say never because there is a little thing called Murphy's Law, and never always happens. You might expect that a thirty year old female patient would be a fairly "easy" patient to take care of, but I find that the patients that come to our floor that are of this fine young age are by far the worst age to take care of as I've mentioned, and just when you feel you've see it all out there, something far more outrageous comes along and outdoes the last ridiculous event, needless to say, having a young individual as part of your days' assignment basically translates into "you are screwed."

Anyway, this young female patient thought she was actually on the catwalk strutting to Right Said Fred's *"I'm too sexy for my shirt, too sexy for my shirt, so sexy it hurts."* Apparently deep down in her heart she thought that she could pull this off and jiggle herself down the hallway buck, and I do mean buck, naked, nipples sticking out flopping all over the place. What the hell gives here? Most people hate looking at themselves let alone staring at another person's "private" zone. It only

152

got worse my dear readers. She was still there when I came back in the morning. I decided to give her the benefit of the doubt until I spent the first 10 minutes of my day with this chick, and I use the term chick loosely.

I was greeted by her nipples when I entered the room and a 70's style coiffe was rearing its ugly head from down below. There was enough hair down there to lay down a carpet in my living room. I didn't even feel confident that a weed wacker could take care of a job this large. The nipples were another story. They were as large as pencil erasers, and they needed to be put back in a jar and stored on a shelf somewhere. She also had an ice pack and heating pack on her head. Slight contradiction wouldn't you think? I'm thinking the heat crosses out the cold, or does the cold interfere with the heat?

She started her admission with a headache and neck ache which somehow developed into an itchy and irritated hoo hoo and hemorrhoids on her ass. She told me the exact medication that she needed for each problem, but threw in to the conversation, "I can't tell what hurts me sometimes." She then proceeded to tell me she couldn't tell the difference between the yeast infection and the hemorrhoids. Honey, it does not take a rocket scientist to tell the difference between your asshole and hoo hoo hole. Two separate holes, two very different parts of your body. Grossly enough, she was in the bed, open wide, scratching

Brenda Wojick

like she was raking the autumn leaves. By golly I believe she found the itch, but the source of the itch was still undetermined.

Kelly suggested that we "get a sample under her finger nails, that will give us a source." EWWW!! And for Christ sakes, put some clothes on those ½ dollars that sit on your chest. It was way too weird to speak to her in my attempt to perform an assessment when I felt as though I was being accosted by a set of pencil erasers. Thankfully, she put a Johnny over her body as she lay in bed, draping it across her. This was just completely inappropriate. She was a young lady but she acted more like a pole dancer at the local strip club. Legs together and clothes on, thank you very much.

I like to think that I gave the M.D. a proper heads up about the patient without being too crude. The doctor came down to fully assess her and figure out what could be going on. One of the questions that he asked her was, "So what brings you here, and what are your symptoms?"

"The usual symptoms of meningitis," was her reply. Who the hell replies like that? It's like she read a medical book, found the symptoms, and that is what she was going to have that day. Girlfriend, you don't want meningitis. It could be a death sentence. Her main complaints are neck pain and headache, and not every pain in the neck is meningitis thank god or I would have had meningitis over 100 times just this year alone. She was in so much pain from a headache that she told the doctor that she will need "50 mg of Demerol Q 4 hours."

Nursing has its own distinct language, and this was nursing speak at its finest. When someone says "Q", it means every. To know that you can receive 50 mg of Demerol every four hours is slightly suspicious, especially when the patient says it like that. PRN is another nursing term, and that means as needed, and she knew this as well. The point of this exercise is that she knew what she wanted and had obviously had enough experience in this situation to get it. I can tell you what I wanted to give her Q 4 hours, a bitch slap, that would have made me happy. She rang her call bell literally every 10 minutes for just about no reason. At 3 hours 59 seconds the call light would go off and she would be looking for her pain medication. She even called my manager stating that I was late giving her, her pain medication. If I could have done a Q 4 hour bitch slap I would be sure not to be late for that event. Actually, I would be early for that one. At 3 hours 58 minutes. *Don't ring the call bell; I'll be waiting outside your door.* I felt like I was neglecting all of my other patients due to her persistent ringing. That was her diagnosis, CHRONIC PAIN IN THE ASS. Maybe a bitch slap was too harsh of a thought. Maybe the M.D. should have prescribed a drive-by cuff of the side of the head Q 4 hours PRN for pain in the ass behavior. At least she would have understood what we were saying.

Speed bump

Occasionally, we do get a good day on our floor where we might have a few minutes to reminisce about our patients and the things that we have had to do over the years. One person came to mind for all of us! We all had the same feeling about this guy because he was downright memorable. He was a quadriplegic and he wheeled around in a motorized wheelchair all the while keeping a pencil in his good hand. He traveled so fast down our hallway like it was a freeway. He was going to hit an elderly person someday right there in the hallway. I told him that I was going to throw out the spike strip in the hallway just to slow him down. I think if there were speed bumps in the hallway he would just fly right over them. He thought I was joking, and I guess that I had to be. This was just the tip of the iceberg.

He had a terrible temper, and there wasn't much that we could do about it, I just felt that we shouldn't always have to deal with it, and we did on a regular basis. He had this undying need to be obsessed with his bowel habits. I have been told that when a person is a quadriplegic

Can You Squeeze My Banana?

they can develop controlling aspects of their behavior. They may focus on things that would not have been an issue if they were not in their situation. He liked to have a BM each and every day. So as part of his plan while he was with us here, he was to receive a suppository to help stimulate his bowels. Then there is the "rectal stimulation" that he enjoyed so much. Every day, he was on the call bell right at the change of shift. First question of the day, "I need you to stimulate my rectum" he said to me.

"You need me to do what?" I immediately made sure that I had cleaned out my ears this morning. I think he told me he wanted me to shove my fingers up his ass. "I'm sorry, excuse me?" I had to double check.

"I need rectal stimulation to help move my bowels," he says as if he is ordering a cheese burger at McDonald's.

"Well, I am not sure that I can do this for you. You did get a suppository this morning and that should help. You might want to give that bad boy a chance." He did not like that answer. He actually began to yell at me. Yelling is not the way to get a girl to stick her fingers up your bum. No dinner, no dancing, just stick it up there. Was he serious??? I had to tell the girls this one. No one could believe it until they were faced with this question when they had to take care of him. We started frantically looking through the policy manual to see if we had to digitally stimulate a patient, or if we got to draw the line

Brenda Wojick

somewhere. For god sakes, draw the line damn it. He needed to focus on something else other than his bowel movements, but he didn't. It became an everyday battle.

He sat in front of the TV with his wheelchair. He had the TV clicker which is also the control for the nurses call bell in his hand. He kept a pencil in his hand, with the eraser pointed down. This was how he pressed the TV control along with the call button, and boy was he obsessed with the call bell, another action that he found he could control. Well guess what? His pencil eraser was finally beginning to wear away. Whoo hoo. This meant that when he went to ring the call bell the pencil slipped and he couldn't press hard enough to hit the button. You may think I am mean, but he is demanding and not very nice to me or any of the staff for that matter. He was a very challenging gentleman to have to work with. As mentioned he liked to drive around the nurse's station all day, circling us when we were trying to work out there. A few times he cut through the nurse's station. I don't know what the hell that was. It's our little sanctuary. We should be enclosed in tinted glass so that no one can see us. But he just came bombing in at any times he felt like. I swear he was taunting us!

So one day he asks for a new pencil. He told me that the eraser was almost gone and he needs a new one. "Oh, I'm sorry; we are all out of pencils today." This was how he constantly rings us for digital

158

Can You Squeeze My Banana?

stimulation and I'm going to give him a new pencil eraser? Who's the crazier person here, me if I gave it to him or him for asking me?

Nappy Nits

It was Thursday, September 27th, and I was working a twelve hour day, which meant that I got to spend half of my productive hours awake and at work. As usual I had a cup of coffee in one hand and a yogurt in the other, and roller blades on my feet to get my day started. I caught wind of a conversation that I wish the wind had blown in the other direction, but of course the nature of the beast is to bite and that exactly what this story does, bite! Then there's the commotion right by the room by the nurse's station. Call me crazy, but when you see the nurse manager, lots of nurses, techs, doctors and infection control, it can't be good, no way, no how!

Everyone modeling their personal protective equipment- cute little blue beanie hats, yellow robes, big ole paper blue surgical boots, gloves and face shields. Tyra Banks, eat your heart out, these bitches look hot. I was curious as hell to find out what in God's name was going on with all the hoopla at the desk, I was scared senseless to even ask because I knew I didn't want to know the answer.

Can You Squeeze My Banana?

I think I heard the word bugs, bugs in the pleural sense as in multiple bugs. It was less than 3 seconds and my whole body became instantaneously itchy. The HAZMAT crew mentioned bugs, but what they actually should have said was infestation. My yogurt went right in the bucket.

The patient was a black guy, homeless and in his 50's, and he was brought into our emergency room department by the cops because the homeless shelter would not accept him. Are you kidding" me? The homeless dude is turned away from the homeless shelter? How the hell does that happen? Someone might want to review their policies and job description because silly me, I thought homeless shelters take homeless people.

He was a tall guy with a nappy appearance. Dred locks were beginning to take form on his head and also his beard. He also had creatures living in his nappy locks. I was told that had maggots, body lice, fleas and other unidentifiable bugs living on him. You could not tell what his actual skin was and what were bugs. His entire body moved. We had no clue. I just remember when I was a kid and yelling out that someone had cooties. Cooties are too cute to have. I would take cooties any day over what this dude had. Everybody was walking by and taking a peek. You just had to see this for yourself. He was a feisty boy too. He would not let anyone touch him or try to shower him. I wanted to vomit. I actually may have, I can't remember.

Brenda Wojick

By now, my hand looked like road rash because I scratched the surface (no pun intended) off of my skin. A couple of flies were seen partying in his room as well, and while this was not bothering the patient, we are all dodging the B-52's that are flying around the nurse's station. They're coming at us like friggin birds, that's how big these damn things are.

In another room my patient was going down for surgery. He did have 10 toes when he left our floor, but he came back with only 9. The nurse's station smelled like poop. Phones were ringing relentlessly, call bells were dinging, bed alarms screamed, people were yelling. I am by far a big mouth hyper girl and I was over stimulated at this point. We had 6 registered nurses, 5 nurse's aides, 4 medical doctors, 3 family members, 2 actual patients and a partridge in a shitty tree.

We were all attempting to handle the day. My patients' call bell went off. It's actually sad, even though this book is not about sad. The only movement this guy had was in his head. He was completely paralyzed. The call bell was taped to his pillow and when he smiled the bell goes off. If he fell asleep and nodded his head, the call bell goes off, sneezed – off, laughed – off, blinked – off again. At this point forensic nursing seemed to be an option. To be a bit more specific, the morgue seemed peaceful. There are no call bells, no family members, no ambulating or toileting. No breathing! How bad could it be? It's quiet! Do you hear that? You shouldn't, there's nothing there.

Can You Squeeze My Banana?

Meanwhile room 12 was walking away on its own. I demand to see my paycheck because I want to see if all this is worth it.

Oil Slick

"A word to the wise ain't necessary -- it's the stupid ones that need the advice"
Bill Cosby

I had to assess this young man in room 19 one Sunday morning in October. He said to me, "I tripped on a piece of oil while I was at the fair."

"A piece of oil, how do you slip on a piece of oil?" I asked.

Can You Squeeze My Banana?

I can see slipping on a piece of "bull" shit while you are at the field, but a piece of oil. How big was that piece of oil? He was now lying in bed practically paralyzed. This was a 37 year old man with more stories and ailments than a 92 year old. I approach his room knowing what I was in for. He's had heart attacks, colon surgery, stab wounds, GERD (acid upset), diverticulitis, post traumatic stress disorder and borderline personality. Anyone who has borderline personality has a very manipulative personality. They attempt to drag everyone in around them on their little ride. Hell, no, I won't go.

Apparently, this dude was at the fair, tripped on a piece of oil, tumbled, hit a few people, went head over heels and ended up on the ground head down. Now he can't move his legs, or so he says. "Can you wiggle your toes," I asked.

"Nope," he said without even attempting to do so.

"Can you move your legs?" I said.

"Nope." Didn't even try. What the hell? It was like he was bored with my questions. He was in so much pain, he just wanted his medications. A little word of advice, if you are paralyzed as he was stating, you would not feel all of that pain that he was saying he had. I touched right in between his toes and the ball of his foot to see what he did. Hell yeah, he wiggled those bad boys right away. Miracle. This would be the first miracle of many.

Brenda Wojick

He was now on the phone with, I believe his wife, and she must have asked, "How are you doing," because his response was, "well, I'm alive." Of course you're alive, you only tripped and fell. For crying out loud, if I walk too fast I trip all the time, should I fall, I get the heck back up again. I left the room for a bit to check on my other patients when we received a phone call on the floor that one of the other floors is missing a six foot tall detoxer with a scraggly beard, and could we please stop him if we see him. I-do-not-think-so. Unless there is a security guard in my pocket when I stop him, it ain't happening. I went back in my dude's room. He was on the phone ordering breakfast and he put the girl on hold. "Yeah, hold on hon my nurse is here. Hi hon." Hon, do I look like a "hon" to you? He covered the phone with his hand and started to order his medications like we were at a McDonald's drive through. "I'll take the Dilaudid now, ahhhh, the Flexeril, the Benadryl, my scheduled Ativan, and then later on I will have the Valium." Holy shit this is just for breakfast. Meanwhile he looked like Puss in Boots from Shrek with the large pupils. He probably couldn't even see me. The valium must be for desert. If I ever took a combination like that you would be singing Amazing Grace at my funeral.

A La Carte

Some days I feel literally like a piece of meat. On one of these days, a twelve hour shift for me, a female patient was admitted to the floor, and god dang, she was moving right in. She was mighty large, weighing in at 400+ pounds, and was bigger than enormous. Enormous was just a teeny, tiny adjective to describe this female patient. The size of her calf muscle was just about the size of my upper thigh. This person was also incredibly demanding on our staff, and her family was just as relentless as she was. They were like rednecks. They were coming over, and they weren't going home. Some had teeth, some did not. Most were overweight and one of them even wore suspenders. No one wears suspenders anymore. It was a busy time at the hospital and the patient was put in a room with 4 beds. We had to move the other patients out. The little old ladies in that room were scared to death. As soon as this female was admitted to our floor for her care her sister moved right in. Supposedly she was her sister-in-law but later on we learned she was just a friend. She demanded a cot and some linen. Was there anything else

Brenda Wojick

I could get this bitch? Finally, a private room was given to the patient and her entire family because it was just too much for the other patients to handle all the commotion. Moving right along...

Her diagnosis was a bleeding rectum and yes, I eventually became her nurse for the day. Why wouldn't I? She became exceedingly demanding, leaning on the call bell every 5 minutes, and her sister followed me around probably about every 20 minutes looking for drinks, food and everything else our tiny little nutrition room might contain. Because of her diagnosis, the patient could only consume clear liquids for her diet. As you might imagine this dietary decision doesn't quite go over so well with this woman who weighs 400 pounds. Damn was she pissed, and now she was pissed at me! I didn't make her rectum bleed, nor did I make her gain so much weight. I am just the nurse, remember, the servant. The only thing that I could picture in my head is the body of a chicken walking into her room with my head sitting right on top of that feathery body; nonetheless, this is exactly what I felt like. I felt like a drumstick when I had to go in there. I actually think I saw her licking her fingertips and smacking her lips every time I entered that room, sizing me up seeing how many bites it would take to get to the center of my bones. She begged me for just about everything that our nutrition room contained. And because of people like her, we actually had to lock up the room. This should not be a hard concept to grasp,

Can You Squeeze My Banana?

or so I thought. Clear liquids consist of liquids that are…CLEAR. She asked for yogurt. "Is that clear," I asked her.

"I'll have an ice cream then," she said.

"No, you won't."

"How about an orange juice?" she said. What part of clear liquid was this chick not getting? Hello! "Clear, clear, clear, things that are see -through are what you can have and absolutely nothing else, nada, nil, nilch. What the cafeteria sends you is what you can have." My kids listen better than this for god sakes.

She would ring, I would go in there, and she would be snoring, with her body oozing off the sides of the bed. It was as if she were melting right into the mattress and leaking onto the floor. There were rolls of skin everywhere, more than I ever cared to see. "I'm in pain", she groaned. She couldn't even wake up fully to tell me this. The doctor came in and was speaking to her, and that's when she began snoring louder than a chainsaw. The second she woke up she asked, "What can I eat, when can I eat?" She was relentless. I told my boss that if she started throwing salt and pepper at me when I walked in the door to her room, I'm outta here. Forget patient safety, I'm protecting myself. I wasn't going to end up in the roasting pan with all the vegetables.

Her sister was a large lady herself, and she would go to the cafeteria and get massive amounts of food and bring it back into the room for to eat. She could feed a third world country with all of that goddamn

169

Brenda Wojick

food. I knew she was giving most of this to her sister. I had to lecture the sister on the importance of not feeding her sister. Hello, she has a little problem called rectal bleed. Not fun. There were empty ring ding and doodles wrappers in the trash can. Who's foolin' who? Hummmm, who do you think is eating all of this crap?

Then her fiancé came in. She has a fiancé. He's about 300+ pounds, but she still has a fiancé. He was telling me, no wait, demanding that I get him some ginger ale. Damn, was he talking to me? There must be someone standing behind me because he better not be speaking to me. My hair was swaying back and forth as I was looking behind me. I calmly explained ever so nicely that we have drinks here for patients only. Well, the patient attempted to lunge forward at me, but we all know that wasn't happening. She lunged from the neck up and that's about it. Sort of like a heave ho motion. HeeeeHeeee. "I fuckin' pay enough being a patient here, get him some gingerale," She spat at me. I was thinking, excuse you, this isn't the hotel Hilton, and I am not room service, and besides did she really need to be an idiot and speak to me like this? I wanted to mutter, go exercise and maybe you wouldn't have weepy, oozing disgusting lower legs where I have to change the bandages because you do not even know what your feet look like. Did I mention that she had no neck either? Her body goes head, shoulders, torso, kankles…(big shins and no ankles). I wonder if at any point in time she realized that her health could be in danger. Dah…

Can You Squeeze My Banana?

Discharge for the patient was a circus show. She didn't want to go. Where else can you lie in bed all day long and do absolutely nothing while being waited on hand and foot, and have your whole damn family come in and eat and drink for free. Who in their right mind would want to leave that precious little deal behind?

It took an entire day to get her out of the hospital, but the time came. To discharge our patients we call transport and have them bring a wheelchair to the patient for safety reasons, but there is no way she was fitting her ass in a standard wheelchair, so we had to bring in the Cadillac of wheelchairs. This is what we call our big wheelchair. It looks like the size of a small futon couch. Two average size people can fit in it comfortably. Even at this point she still wouldn't get her ass off of the bed. My suggestion was to dangle a sirloin steak in front of her, perhaps on a piece of string and lead her to the wheelchair. She was eventually wheeled down the hallway with her shirt raised so high it was like a belly shirt from the bad 80's generation. She also had on tight leggings. Wow, what a sight as she left. Good riddance and have a good day.

My "Titty" is Stuck

"Laughter is higher than all pain"

Elburt Hubert

One of my coworkers needed assistance down at the end of the hallway. She had a very large female patient, and by large I mean 400+ lbs, yes again. On this hospitalization, because she was a frequent flyer, she had eczema and dermatitis from head to toe. Her face was peeling, her ears were a peeling mess, her skin was all red, dry and flaky, the odor was furious and she was the largest woman I have ever come in contact with. Have you ever seen flaky Italian pastry? If you saw her, you would never eat it again, I guarantee you. She had layers of skin on her sheets, the floor, and her hair. It was like she was a snake shedding her skin but not in one piece. Oh my god doesn't sum it up. Why me? Why anyone?

She was wedged tightly into the side of her bed. Picture 400 lbs dripping in between the mattress of the bed and the railing on the side. Her boobs were practically hitting the floor. She had these big ole floppy breasts. I never in my entire life saw anything of this magnitude. The tip of her nipples were swinging on the floor like a pendulum. Her stomach, which we know is a panis, was seeping onto the floor. She was like a pile of mud; I hate to say, plopping everywhere.

The stench, oh the stench, what can I say about it? It was so bad I had to wear two masks when I entered the room to go help the rest of my coworkers. She was screaming and yelling at the very top of her lungs, good lord. I was talking with a few nurses and one of the doctors on the floor, when a nasty stench floating by. The doctor sniffed, and I didn't want him to think it was me. It was a yeasty smell, a bad infection smell, and it was her. On top of the red patches, she had a yeast infection. You know where females get yeast infection, in the hoo hoo region. Well she had one there, and all over her body. She was even oozing from her eyes. We could probably use her to bake some bread she had so much yeast. (That gives you a bad visual I'm sure) She needed to be sent through the car wash to be hosed down. Two masks just wasn't cutting it. We needed to move her, and we needed a miracle. I was waiting for the sky to open up above us and Mother Nature to show her face and say, "here, let me help you." Instead, four more nurses came into the room. That must have been the voice I heard. We now needed a fork lift. You really need to get a visual on the size of the nurses and then the size of this woman and realize, this is not going to happen. I was not going to rip my arm off because someone couldn't control their

Brenda Wojick

eating habits. There had to be eight of us in there from nurses to nursing assistants and the big question on everyone's mind was, "how the hell are we going to pull this one off?"

We began by taking the sheets off of the bed so that we could use them as a hoist. We also had to peel her out from the side of the bed, and she did leave some of her skin behind. Someone, not me, peeled her boobies off the floor and put them back on her chest right where they should be, and the best part was picking up her stomach and flipping it onto the bed where it belongs- on her, not the floor. Little by little the staff was grabbing those little masks, just like the two that I had on over my face. It's a good thing that I had something good for lunch because I had to mouth breath behind that mask. Someone moved her prematurely and a skin flap moved, and I gagged so loudly I wish I could describe to you the sound that came from my mouth. I had to walk away and make sure that I didn't throw up in my mask. It would have gone right back up through my nose. It would have been a disaster, still a disaster better than the one I was to endure.

One of the nurses was attempting to peel her arm out from the side rail, and the patient was just not having it. She was actually pulling the nurse down on the bed with her. EEEwww! Nasty! She would have drowned in the flubber. We pulled her out just in time. "On the count of three, take a deep breath," Kathy said to the patient. "Don't anybody else take a deep breath though, only the patient." I cried. Of course I

174

had to say that. Kathy began the count. "One, two, three!" She went nowhere. She didn't even budge. Eight people and a big sheet and the female patient didn't even budge. She hollered and screamed so loudly that everyone on the third floor must have heard, and I hope no one needed any staff out at the nurse's station because everyone and their relative was in the last room on the left attempting to flip the burger over. For goodness sakes, we have to lift, pull, roll and let down. We had to do this. It was taking way to long. "Put me down, put my head up, help!" she's screaming. No matter how many times we told her to shhhh and calm down, it's going to be okay, she screamed that much louder. Finally, we all got up enough oomph and picked up the sheet and rolled her way the heck over, only to see that she had been on that side for so long, like a log, she rolled right back over into the hole on the side of the bed that she started out on. Ugh! My job is done here!

Father's Day salute

I had a rather large gentleman that I was taking care of one day. He really didn't do much. He just lay in bed with no ambition to get any better, and all he wanted to do was sleep, oh yeah, and eat. This story really does not have anything to do with him; it's his wife that was extremely strange.

The patient was in his room sleeping because from what I can remember is he hadn't slept much that night, and let's face it; the hospital is not where you get your best rest to begin with. Anyway, he had finally fallen asleep at roughly noon time, and this is when his wife decided to pay him a visit. What was different about this day was that it was Father's Day. Unless you're a father, it is not your day! She approached the nurse's station and asks for his nurse. Hello, that would be *moi*. I go up to the front to chat with this disheveled looking female in her sixties. "How's he doing?" She asked me.

"You can go down there and take a peek," I said sweetly.

"He's sleeping; I don't want to bother him," was her reply. I'm thinking, why the hell did you even come in here? Who knows how long he will be sleeping for? Unbeknownst to me, there was a hidden ulterior motive. She then asked, "Can I get a free meal sent down there for me while I'm waiting?" She wouldn't be waiting for anything if she would just wake him up.

"I'm sorry; we do not have free meals that we can order," I said politely, figuring that was the end of story. Nope, she had to go on. "It's Father's Day, they should give us free lunch," she said.

Now, I don't ever remember Father's Day being that big of a holiday that we offer free meals. We don't even offer free meals to the sick fathers on the floor, and besides, she ain't no father. Why was she trying to get the free meal?

"This is ridiculous; we should get a free meal on father's day," She repeated.

I said, "Well, I can offer you a voucher if you would like."

Can You Squeeze My Banana?

"How much is a voucher?"

"It's $5.00." Well, she didn't like that answer. She felt that she could walk down to the cafeteria for less money than that. "You can go down to the café and get what you would like," I told her, "but quite frankly, it will not be less than $5.00."

"Nah, I don't want to do that."

I felt like saying, suit yourself. This was not my problem. I have my lunch in the fridge out back for god's sake. I didn't have to worry about what she was going to eat today, and quite frankly it's not my concern. I had a job that I need to go finish now. This lady only had one thing on her mind and it was feeding her very large belly. Never mind the fact that her husband had a horrible night and that was why he was sleeping. None of her questions revolved around his care other than the initial question of, "how's he doing?" The thought of him was long gone. This lady was on a mission, a mission for food.

Just as I was about to sneak away, she came up to me and spoke out of the side of her mouth as if to tell me a secret, "Can you get me one of the sandwiches in the lunch room that you give to patients?"

Is she for real? "Ma'am, I'm sorry, but those are for the patient's only."

"Can't you just say it's for a patient and get me one?"

Why had she not eaten lunch before she got here? She was making my life miserable because she could not get a free sandwich, but I was

177

Brenda Wojick

going to stand my ground. Had the circumstances been different and I really felt there was a reason to give away a sandwich, believe me, I would. This lady was just trying to get a free bee. The whole way here she must have planned this. I said, "No I can't. I'm sorry. Those sandwiches are there for patient's snacks, especially the diabetics on the floor who need to eat when they have low blood sugar." Why the hell was I even explaining this to this chick? It is none of her business.

"They won't even miss one," she says to me. What I wanted to say was, *They sure will if they are on the floor in a comatose state because we could not get any nutrition into them because that lady ate your sandwich.* "I apologize ma'am; I cannot get one of those." This is more like what I said. She stormed away saying, "Its Father's Day, I can't believe I can't get a sandwich around here." I wanted to yell at her, *You ain't no one's daddy!*

Just when I thought it was over, it wasn't. It was medication time, and I had to go down to this gentleman's room to give him his pills. When I walked in he was sound asleep and snoring loudly. His lovely wife was sitting at his side devouring his tray that was sent up from the kitchen. When I walked in, she said, "Oh, don't wake him up. Let him sleep." Of course she wouldn't want me to wake him up. Naturally, I did. He took his pills and literally fell right back to sleep. When he was starting to come to and she was licking her chops from eating his meal, she asked him if he wanted to eat, and then she proceeded to call and

178

Can You Squeeze My Banana?

get him another tray for lunch. Do you know what? She got her way in the end, and I got this story.

Undertoe

When I was younger, my mother always told me not to go in the water past my hips at the beach because there was a really bad under toe out there. I was scared as a kid, and rightfully so. Little did I know that 25 years later I would be afraid of that same under toe that was about to sneak up on me.

This particular day I had floated to another floor, and it was no joke when they told me I was down in the "hole." This hole was the patient's rooms that were way down the end of the hallway, and each room had four patients in them. The first room I was taking care of had three female patients that were in there. The walk down there alone felt as if it were uphill the entire way with absolutely no end in sight. Once I made it to the room, there was that serious under toe and it took me by surprise and dragged me in much deeper than I had ever imagined. I'm gasping for air, and I can't breathe. This was not going to be a good day.

In a situation such as this, guaranteed there is always a ring leader to the group, and sure enough, I found out which one that was. I went in that room at 7:30 and I swear I didn't get out of there until 3:00. One of them would ask for something, the other patient wants your full attention so they yell over to you, by then the third female is feeling unloved and is also begging for attention. One wants salt, one wants cream, and the third wants a new Depends. The leader was rallying up her troops. I couldn't even ask them a question without her answering. She knew all of their illnesses, all their aches and pains. She had them pull all their curtains back so that she could see, hear and talk to them all.

As I leaned over to take care of one of the ladies, on the other side of the curtain is this 79 year old lady who yelled out, "Oh shit, I dropped my f…ing water." God, is she someone's nana? She totally had a potty mouth. She had a very raspy voice from years of smoking. This sweetie pie told me what she wanted and when she wanted it. If she could stand tall and proud she probably tops the charts at 4 feet 10 inches tall, but boy is she rough. She was not putting up with the ring leader's crap. The ring leader was the lady in A bed closest to the door. She was taking control of all the other beds, B, C and D. Anyway, she attempted to make conversation to the biker babe in B bed, but biker babe wasn't having it. The ring leader was a frequent flyer here at the hospital. All she had to do was pay attention to other people's problems. Biker babe in B bed was also a frequent flyer. The bad thing was that they were both in the same room. Good thing was, they both couldn't walk. There would be no beat downs today. By the next day it got better.

Brenda Wojick

Day 2 of my punishment, A bed went home and a new patient went into A bed and B bed went into C bed so that they were diagonally across from each other. The lady in A bed was a 90 year old, 90 pounds soaking wet, frail but spunky, old biddy. She was yelling, "I have nothing to live for." As a good nurse I took a chance and asked, "Why do you have nothing to live for? What is wrong?" With such anger and vengeance she belted out, "I can't find my Fixodent!" It was difficult to console her because I wanted to laugh, but no sooner did I compose myself, than the biker babe in C bed started screaming, "Get over here quick. I need you now!" Aww, could she love me that much? Did she appreciate my being her nurse? Nah! She then starts yelling, "I need to take a shit, get me the bedpan. Quick, hurry." Now if that's not breakfast talk then I don't know what is. "Ooohhh, Aahh, hurry the hell up. Quick before I go in my bed." You could tell that back in her day she was a tough muffin and no one messed with her. Just the way she screamed for the bedpan had me scared. I was in my own damn frazzled state of mind now. I scrambled for the stupid bedpan that wasn't where it is supposed to be at the side of her bed. I turned her, moved her, and picked her up looking for it. "Jesus Christ, watch what you're doing," She yelled. What I was doing was trying to get this chick on the darn bedpan so I do not have to change the sheets. I finally got her on, and she sat there for a good 20 minutes. You could hear her moan all the way down by the nurse's station. She used the call bell, and I went down there. "I can't

Can You Squeeze My Banana?

friggin go. Get this damn thing outta here," she told me. I wondered if she would be missed if I got rid of her along with the bedpan. Do you know what the scariest thing about his whole situation was? She was a registered nurse back in her day. I sure as hell hope she was much more sympathetic than she was and is now because I don't think the lady in A bed could survive any more of this madness. Hell, I can't deal with the madness, but I do. This makes it a good day!

All in a Day's Work

When all hell breaks loose on the floor, and there is more chaos than usual, I start to question the moon. Yes, the moon that sits high above us shining down from the deep black sky.

Some days I just want to work and get over with the day. I don't want to laugh. This day was one of those days. One of my patients was leaping out of bed the second I got onto the floor. She was obviously a confused elderly female, but I've had this patient before, and this was not her normal state of mind. She was usually a very pleasant, cutie patootie pants, but not for long. Then she turned into the devil.

If anyone had a camera, this would have been the perfect photo opportunity. I wouldn't have been able to smile because my head was jammed between the door that was against the wall, and squeezed under the armpit of my patient. I still wonder how I got myself into this predicament. This situation was a no brainer. I got up on this day and got the Hulk for my patient. Someone, I can't remember who, saw the situation unfold and yelled over to me, "Should I call a Team one?"

Can You Squeeze My Banana?

Calling a Team One brings security, nurses, physicians and the psych department, usually for patients who get agitated and might need to be restrained. Well, now let me think about this. My brain is against the door, and my patient is ready to pummel me, so, sure, call a Team One. "Team one," I said in my muffled little voice.

Although she was about 72 years old (don't laugh) age does not matter when you have dementia. These people become very strong and powerful. I don't know what takes over their mind, but they will crush you. She stood about 5'10" and was probably 190 pounds, senile and demented, and those terms are not used lightly. It is actually a very sad situation because this lady had no clue where she was or who she was. She was living in the past, she saw unusual things, and she was violent. She was actually on my floor because she tried to stab someone at her nursing home with a fork. Our psychiatric floor was over flowing, so someone came up with the bright idea to admit her to the medical surgical floor, no physical symptoms, only behavioral. We are not equipped for this type of behavior although we are starting to see more and more confused behavior on the floor we work on and not by choice.

She had a 1:1 sitter for her protection so that she did not hurt herself or anyone else for that matter. The person assigned to that job needs to be right by the patient's side at all times. It is a very grueling job, especially if the patient will not sit down for one second. That was the

Brenda Wojick

case here, so thank you Kelly. She paced for seven out of the eight hours of our shift. She walked by the nurse's station trying to grab our charts, asking, "What are these doing here? I want one." I redirected her so many times I didn't know what direction I was going. I crushed up her medication and gave it to her in apple sauce which she took, much to my surprise. "Ahhhh, that tastes kilty," she responded. Not sure what kilty was, but I didn't care what it tasted like, she took the damn thing. "Over there, we can't, who are you, psstt. Bring it because, yeah. I said and pick it up." This was a typical conversation that she and I had all day long. Then clear as day, she was looking at a magazine, ripping out pages to keep her busy. She looked at me and the tech and said, "oh, Denzel." Sure enough, Denzel Washington was in the picture.

Any whoo, she was a tough one to keep up with. She walked too darn fast that the tech, and myself when I was needed, had to jog to keep up with her. I could just picture her making a run for the door. Well, she did better than that, she got me. She was having another outburst in the hallway when she just snapped! She slipped behind a nurse and came busting in to the medication room, which is kept locked at all times. It scared the shit right out of me. I got her into the hallway so that we could handle her in a more open setting. The bigger the space the better, so I could run if need be. I think she was yelling "no" when I approached her. She was starting to fling her arms in every direction. Everyone who was involved with restraining her were a lot smaller than she was. We grabbed her arms so that she wouldn't punch us, but she did better. She got a hold of my arms so tight that the tech was unable to rip her off of me. From that position, she got my head twisted under her arm so that I was squished up against the door. All you could hear was my voice, "Oh, god. Help." This was about the point when someone mentioned calling a Team One.

It felt like it took everyone forever and a day to get there. Thirty seconds may have well been thirty hours. I wish someone was able to get a snapshot of what I looked like with my head against the wall, now that everything was okay of course. Everyone told me that I looked like a little head coming off of her body, because they couldn't see my body since I was stuck behind her. The poor thing ended up in four point restraints until they could work briskly at her departure to the senior adult unit. See, a little head football and we can get her transferred to where she needs to be. I took one for the team!

Hello, and welcome to Wal-Mart

I had no idea what was in store for me or the entire unit, but somehow I knew that by the end of the day I wanted to be a Wal-Mart greeter, someone who sits at the front door and says, "Hi, welcome to Walmart." Huge cut in pay, but today that doesn't seem to bother me what-so-ever. Right after my patients' colostomy bag burst all over the place I felt that I could take a cut in pay and hit the road for a new job.

187

Brenda Wojick

I had two very unique patients, one gentleman who was unfortunately deaf, which puts me at a disadvantage, and a 77 year old female who is doing the detox deed. She is someone's mother, sister, grandmother, but for me, she is my patient, and I am to care for her throughout my shift. It sounds a lot easier than it really was. She originally checked herself into a recovery program but her shortness of breath bought her a one way ticket to the hospital. I performed my usual admission assessment to find out that this was just the beginning of her detox period. She had only been at the other program for a very short period of time, less than 24 hours. Someone usually starts withdrawing terribly after the third day without having a drink. This rule applies whether you have one drink or ten drinks. This duo was going to be challenging.

Coffee, yogurt, va jay jay, three things that do not mix well together, especially first thing in the morning. "Can someone close that door over there, really," I asked. I will have you know that coffee time in the morning is very sacred, and there is nothing more disturbing than drinking coffee with a vagina staring back at you. As I tried to shake off the image, I realized we had nursing students on our floor working with us. We are trying to teach them the proper way to care for a patient, their patient, our patient. I always say to them, "Treat them as if he/she was your mother or father, brother or sister." Shit, if my mother or father acted like this who knows what I would do. There was no way on this earth that I could picture my mother to be like this particular lady. She

188

has her legs up and over her head. Damn, I can't do that and I'm half her age. Shockingly, I was jealous. Her Johnny followed up her long legs and continued over her torso and continued to cover her head, and we all know that we don't have matching underwear to the Johnny we provide. Technically she was showing everyone in the hallway her hoo hoo. This is not so mortifying to me as it is to the brand new nursing students, many of them who are male. I just shook my head but they cringed as if they were in pure agony. They didn't know what the hell to make of this.

Meanwhile, down the hallway and to the left, I was working with two techs who called the secretary to say, "We need Brenda down here now." *Oh no, why?* I'm thinking to myself. If they needed me immediately, it couldn't be good. Oh god, I was right. This was not good. The patient's colostomy bag exploded! Poop bath for everyone. It just wouldn't stop… The stench was unbearable. His bag broke and poop just kept coming out of it. Under a colostomy bag is a stoma. That is the part of your intestine that protrudes from your skin. His actually appeared herniated. It was a like a little head sticking out of his stomach looking back at us. We removed the pouch because it did have to be changed now. His stoma was oozing like a volcano. We couldn't get it to stop, nor could I get the smell to go away. Under both of my masks I had to twist 2X2 gauze and stuff it way up my nostrils to help me get through this ordeal.

Mr. Doctor

"The easiest job in the world has to be <u>coroner</u>*. Surgery on dead people. What's the worst thing that could happen? If everything went wrong, maybe you'd get a pulse"*
Dennis Miller (quoted in Underground Humor, 1997, ed: Edward Bergin)

Why did this guy keep calling me? I couldn't get anything done. He was being awfully persistent about his wife's discharge. She was more than able to speak for herself, yet he wanted every single detail about her impending discharge. Why wasn't he calling her looking for information? Maybe he thought he was going to receive some secret information, that I must have been withholding this "top secret" agenda. Cut me some slack, I have other patients here to look after. This was just the first phone call of many.

"Brenda to the nurse's station." That was the sound of the intercom. "Yes," I asked as I poked my head out the door. "Family phone call,"

Can You Squeeze My Banana?

the secretary yelled to me. I shuffled out and picked up the line. "This is Brenda, how can I help you?"

"This is Doc Dolittle (you will see why I call him this) Helen's husband. Any word on her discharge?" He clearly referred to himself as Doc, not doctor but Doc.

"Not at this time, but as soon as I hear anything I will be sure to let her know right away." He came back with, "Well, she may not understand what you are saying to her, so I want to be there when you discharge her."

This lady was very oriented, she was not an idiot, she could process discharge instructions, I'm sure. "I'm a doctor, and I would prefer if I could be there," her husband continued. "That's fine," I answered, "probably in a couple of hours we will be able to get her on her way."

"I'll call you back," he said. Why? Why the hell did he have to call me back? His wife was not retarded, but she just might be for marrying him. Just kidding. He meant well.

Then I heard it again over the intercom: "Brenda to the nurse's station." Oh *for the love of god*. Once again I sat down and picked up the phone. "This is Brenda, how can I help you?" I said.

"Hi, it's Doc Dolittle. Are you Helen's nurse?" Okay, well I answered the phone the same way one hour ago, *this is Brenda how can I help you?* He was missing something here. Naturally, I did not say this, but I really wanted to. "Yes, this is Brenda, Helen's nurse."

Brenda Wojick

"Did I speak to you earlier?" he asked.

"Yeeessss, you did, what can I do for you?" I said very nicely.

"Is she ready to go?" I suggested that he might come up and wait with her and she would be ready to go shortly.

Eventually he arrived, and introduced himself. "Hi, I'm Dr. Dolittle, so what's going on with Helen," he asked.

"Well, she needs some follow up appointments, and she is going home with some prescriptions."

"What were her ACP and CBC?" (Acute care profile which are your electrolytes and complete blood count which are your red and white blood cells) Most people don't ask questions like this meaning non-layman's terms. "They were normal," I muttered. "What was her H & H?" (Hemoglobin and Hematacrit) Who the hell would ask this? Unless you are in the medical field, you have no clue as to what this is. Most people would say, "How's her blood?" I glared at him as I replied, "her blood is within normal limits."

"Now I want you to show me how to give Helen her Lovenox shot," he said.

"Okay." I got ready to demonstrate this and he busted out the terminology again. "Do we have to check her PT/INR?" (clotting factor) Oh jeez here we go. If you know we have to check it when a person is on Lovenox then do it. I said, "Yes, you do."

192

Can You Squeeze My Banana?

"Is that with a sub Q (subcutaneous) needle?" He asked. Okay, I got the point, you are a smarty pants, and you obviously have a job in the medical field. "So, given the fact that you understand all the medical mumbo jumbo, do you work in the medical field?" I asked with a big smile on my face. "I'm a physician," he replied.

"Oh, what type of medicine do you practice?"

He said, "I'm a vet."

"I'm sorry, did you say vet, as in veterinarian?" I asked.

"Yes, I'm a retired veterinarian." I'm swapping lingo with a retired vet. Now, that is a wonderful profession, and I am not saying that it isn't, I'm just stating things are a bit different here, say two less legs, and a lot less fur. I'm laughing because many family members that come in who are doctors, nurses, lawyers keep it to themselves unless absolutely necessary. He was too eager to spit the terminology. I just wanted to give instructions and have him be on his merry way. She was a complete pleasure to have; he, on the other hand needed to go back into retirement.

Familiar Pain

I had a pain, a really bad one, and it happened to be in my ass. It was sharp, it was shooting, and it also had a name, a name that I cannot give to you now or at any time, but I can tell you it was bothersome and wicked. There was nothing I could do that would get rid of this troublesome pain. I couldn't shake it off or massage it out, it still remained the same. Unfortunately for me it lingered here for two days, causing me discomfort every step of the way throughout my day. Maybe it was a thorn in my side masking itself as a pain in my ass, either way; no matter what term I used it didn't go away.

On Wednesday I made a desperate plea for this pain to not torture me. Damn it all, no such luck. Just when I had visions of throwing in the towel to only round one in this boxing match, a reliable source, a little birdie if you will, informed me my day would actually be great. The estimated time of my "pain's" dissipation is 5:00 pm. I was one of the happiest little boxers that day.

Can You Squeeze My Banana?

If you haven't guessed it by now, my pain in the ass had a gender and that gender is male. He was admitted all the way down the hall in room five, not too close but for this day it had proven to be significantly too far indeed, but there was an angel on my side looking out for me. It sounds impressive but in reality it was the doctor blessing me with the information that my pain should resolve soon. Naturally, I was elated by this simple piece of information. There was going to be a happily ever after ending to this story. It was a shame because he was really a nice enough dude, kind and friendly. I couldn't really ask for anything more in a patient. He was young, 36 years old. When the patient is young, it's like their vacation time, and I'm their cruise director here to make their stay much more pleasurable. I am anything but that person. I am here to follow doctor's orders and assist them in assisting you feel better so you can stand on your own two feet and be on your merry little healthy way.

Putting personality aside, I am going to mention appearance. Shallow perhaps, but necessary. Having a visual helps any story. He had a tiny head, massive size body, and when he was in bed you could never see a head sticking out there at all, but you could hear a voice and a stream of questions that echoed in his room and in my head all day long.

"Could I have a pitcher of water?" he bellowed out.

Brenda Wojick

"Of course you can." This was my comeback answer. That was an easy request, no fear here, until the stream of questions was steadily flowing with no end in sight. It never ended with just one pitcher of water. Just as I returned to his room and set down the pitcher of water, he asked, "Can I have a cup of ice?" "Sure," I said. I moseyed back down the hallway towards the floor's tiny nutrition room, got the ice, and headed back. "Here ya' go, I'll be back down to check on you shortly." Who knew shortly would be now. What the hell man?

"Can you unhook my IV so I can go to the bathroom?"

I said to him, "you can just wheel it with you so this way it doesn't have to be unhooked all the time."

"I can't wheel it all the way over there."

Was he kidding me? Over there was 20 feet away. Oh for god sakes bed – bathroom, bathroom – bed. He was not the most physically fit gentleman, but 15 – 20 feet isn't exactly strenuous exercise. If I had to unhook every person that was connected to an IV drip I would never get anything done. I would be assigned to one patient at all times. It was bad enough I couldn't get anything done today. I could feel the anxiety building.

"Now can I have something for pain?" Could he not tell me this ages ago when I first started on this journey that I never asked for? There is no doubt that he is 300 pounds. The next question was, "Why can't I eat?" Uhmmm, let's pick this question apart, and for all of you

196

Can You Squeeze My Banana?

non-healthcare personnel reading this, perhaps you too can figure it out. He was on vacation somewhere in Mexico eating, drinking and apparently happy. Remember the saying, "Don't drink the water in Mexico?" Everyone knows that, but apparently he ignored that. On his way home from vacation he became violently ill with vomiting and diarrhea. Now he had been rewarded with a luxurious 2 night 3 days stay at his community hospital. His prizes included remaining NPO (nothing by mouth), which meant, no water and no food. But he did get to have an IV drip of normal saline for his vacationing pleasure. As a bonus, he would also be bunking in with an older gentleman twice his age who was hearing impaired so he too could listen to the show the old gentleman was watching whether he liked it or not.

Let's discuss attire, shall we? I usually like my patients to wear some form of clothing, whether it be a Johnny or their own pants and shirt. I am not picky just grateful. When some patients get here they feel that clothing is optional, and that is not the case. There was no nudity with this man, otherwise I would not know how I would react, but he was not wearing a shirt, and I thought he had a pair of black shorts on until he made his way to the bathroom one of his many times. It is then I noticed a flap in the front of the shorts. Shorts do not have flaps in the front, nor are they usually form fitting. Oh good lord, they were boxer briefs. I mean, I know that underwear are made for people of all shapes and sizes and I don't know what I was thinking, but I had never ever

Brenda Wojick

seen a pair of underwear this size, and I've seen a lot here at work. If the underwear were this big, I wanted to see the size of the package that they came out of. The flap in the front was as big as my head, and this is not where I would want it to be, but I'm just saying.

"I'm in a lot of pain, do you think I can get some Vicodin," he whined.

"Sure, do you want one or two? This is how the doctor ordered it depending on how bad your pain is." He told me he would have two just in case. Off I went and retrieved two of the Vicodin. This way I figured he would take a nice little nappie poo after his pain medicine. I brought it down to him, and he told me, "I'm not going to take the second one now. I've changed my mind." I brought myself back down to the medication room and put the other Vicodin away to only come out of the medication room to once again find his call bell going off. I could feel my face turning colors and my temperature rising. I knew he was going to ask for the next Vicodin. I scurried all the way down the hall to his room. "On second thought, I am going to have the other Vicodin." Of course he is. Without a doubt this sucked. As I once said, the younger they are, the needier they get. As part of his physical therapy and weight management plan, I should have given him the code so that he could go down and get his own Vicodin.

TEAM ONE

When I leave for work in the morning, I should not really have to worry about danger or getting hurt in any way. I would like to leave that to the other professionals such as the boxers, wrestlers, cops and correction officers.

"Whose butt is this," I asked as I pointed to some man's derriere sticking out from under the nurse's station. His head was tucked under the counter. His cane was holding his torso up and he used it like it was a vacuum cleaner. His ass was sticking high up in the air almost as if he was hiking the football back to Tom Brady. He was picking up every imaginary dust bunny there was on our desk and on the floor. He was even talking to the little imaginary dust bunnies. One of the nurses told me this was the good patient of the night. They just let this gentleman sit at the nurse's station to keep him happy and calm. We tend to do that with the demented patients. The quieter they are, the better. We don't always have any other alternative when it comes to difficult patients. We piece our care plan together and hope it flies. When we do let a patient

Brenda Wojick

hang in the nurse's station there is also a sense of invasion, a distinct realization that they are in the "nurses" territory, our territory. This is our domain, our casa, not me casa es su casa. For the eight to twelve hours we are there we should not have to share our space with anyone, and I mean anyone.

So I was enthralled with the report that I was hearing from the night staff. I was the charge nurse for the floor for the day, so I had the opportunity to hear about all of the patient's conditions. If something were to happen during the course of the day, I would be aware of it. Other than the "good patient" hanging out with us, we had another guy in four point restraints tied to his bed close by. The reason for his hospitalization was change in mental status. Do ya think? I do mean that very sarcastically. He was Rocky Balboa in the boxing ring, or so he thought, except Apollo Creed was not with him. He was attempting to beat the daylights out of the night manager and one of the male nurses on the floor. Then two security guards jumped into the 'ring'. What a thrill. I almost wish I had witnessed this.

Uh oh! Suddenly the bunny watcher had become a computer programmer. I must interject to tell you that this guy was a large gentleman. He had to be at least 6 feet tall, over 250 pounds and strong as hell. Our floor had all new computers just recently installed for some charting changes. He decided to take it upon himself to tinker with the plug. First he was touching the wire, harmless enough,

200

Can You Squeeze My Banana?

but them he moved onto the outlet. When we didn't let him proceed with his actions, he tipped over our new computer. First some of the staff attempt to reason with him. Hah…as you can imagine this was not going too well. You cannot reason with the demented. He became more agitated. We needed him calm. He was out in the middle of the floor for everyone to see and hear, but at the same time the tipped over computer was a reminder of what he can do. I had just started my day. It was barely 8am. "Call a TEAM ONE." This entails a team of people from IV therapy, psychiatry, security, charge nurse, nurse in charge of the patient, and the nurse manager. "I'm not going back to my room," he was screaming. "Why don't we just take you back there so you can relax," someone tried to coax.

"Noooooo." The doctor that was taking care of him today is an awesome doctor who takes great care of his peeps, but he was not thinking rationally at this time.

"Just let him sit there and do his thing."

"I don't think so," I snapped. "He's been sitting there all night tinkering and picking at the air. Now he's done it. The dude is tipping over computers. We can't let him sit there." Meanwhile, security was practically wrestling him to the ground. It was actually quite entertaining. The patient was most definitely giving them a run for their money. He was fighting like a bull. He was not giving in. The psych staff just stood there. Hello, your role is? Can you say Haldol? I can, at least 2 mg of it.

Brenda Wojick

5 mg would be better. The doctor got a hold of the patient's daughter on the phone and they put the combative patient on the phone with her. Boy did he ever change his tune. She was reaming him from the sound of their phone conversation. Yes, she could put an end to this frustrating standoff. The funniest thing ever was when he was being brought back into his room, the guy that was restrained pulled his entire body up so that he could sneak a peek of the melee. He was trying with all of his might to release himself from the bed. It ain't happening. The patient was finally brought back to his room where he fell asleep for the rest of the entire day. Not a bad idea right now.

Thanksgiving Day

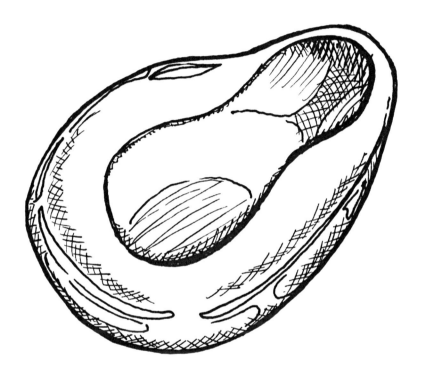

My eyes, as well as everyone else's on the third floor, were burning. The complaints were piling in from staff members and family members. For a brief minute I actually felt like it was my fault. I am giving you fair warning; do not eat while you are reading this chapter. You will

Brenda Wojick

without a doubt lose it. If I could have foreseen the mass destruction that was about to take place on my shift....I almost made it out this day with a quiet shift behind me, on time and unscathed, but I should have known better. What I should have also realized was I was going to need a very high pair of goulashes, a shovel and a rain slicker. I went by the door, peaked in and caught a glimpse of the patient's eyes as he said, "I defecated." I actually love that word defecate. It's such a fancy way to say, 'I shit myself'.

"Okay," I said. "I'm going to get your cleaned up. Let me go grab some things." His cute little response was, "Nah, I'm going to stay like this. I'm just gonna shit myself again anyways." I was sure he would, and yes, I would have liked to take him up on his generous offer of leaving him be, but there was no possible way I could let him sit in that toxic waste. Meanwhile, throughout the entire conversation he sat in his own feces and the smell literally escaped from the confines of his own room. It quickly permeated the air in the hallway and took hold like a dense fog would engulf a small lake. It was a short lived battle, and the foul odors won by encompassing the hallway that surrounded his room. It began outside his room and became immediately noticeable at the nurse's station. This was not a difficult task because the RN's station is situated directly across from his room. Gross! I waited for the sounds of emergency alarms as they would scream as if we were in a war torn country alerting us of a biochemical situation, but there

204

were no bells. This situation had not happened to me in a while, so why today on Thanksgiving Day? The complaints were overwhelming. When something reeks that badly, does one realize he or she reeks? Can they stand themselves? Often times I think not because this guy was as happy as a pig in shit. (This comparison was intended) Kim came to get me to tackle the problem, which was a lot larger than I had originally anticipated. This was not a normal diaper change. The mess was so large it was seeping from the sheets. The two of us took a peek under the blanket and my eyes immediately watered and I may have cried. In fact, I did cry, sobbed is much more like it. You would too if you were me. I had never felt so lost; we literally had no idea where to begin.

He finally agreed to let us change him, and I was wondering if I could change my mind just like he did. What he lay in resembled brown foam, like something that washed up on the shore line of Revere Beach. It was bubbling, and at this point I feared for the patient's safety. I thought he would drown if he went under. This was not an unrealistic surmise.

Once in, I never thought I would come out. I ran towards the door and cried for help, those who could run bolted in the direction away from me, and I've got to tell you, I didn't blame them. Others may not have "heard me." Nonetheless, there was a float tech that came to our rescue. Yay! We were not stranded on Shit Island after all. I will try to spare you with every tiny horrible unnecessary grotesque detail because

Brenda Wojick

quite frankly I cannot bear to relive this, but for the sake of the book, I will. What bothered me the most was that I could not even think about the nice Thanksgiving Day turkey dinner that I was going home to. This shit fest was interrupting my pleasant yummy holiday thoughts.

We began to conquer the mess, just the three of us. I almost lost consciousness, but what woke me up and made me jump as if I were on fire was when we rolled this guy to the left side and rolled the sheet a teeny tiny spec of poo, microscopic in size, but still, hit the lower part of my green thermal long sleeve shirt that I wear under my scrub top to keep me warm. It fell in the region right before you hit the cuff of my sleeve. Looking back, the poo shot was so tiny you could barely see it with the naked eye, but I knew it was there and to me it looked like the biggest shit blob ever. All I knew was I did not want it there whether it was big or small. I was frantic. I came running from the room gagging at first. My stomach muscles were pulling tightly as I was trying with all my heart and soul not to hurl on the floor in front of the patient's room. I thought this was going to be a total disaster. I couldn't even think about the little patient, it was all about me right about now. The moment had passed and no sawdust needed to be sprinkled on the floor. I commenced running after I regained my composure, my sleeve in my hand, stretching it out so that there was never any hope for that shirt. I remember yelling, "Cut it, cut it!" The girls at the front desk were looking horrified, but to me this was an emergency. "Get the scissors

Can You Squeeze My Banana?

and cut my damn shirt." No one knew what to make of my shrilling cry for help. "Get the scissors." I said to one of the nursing assistants, "and cut off the wrist of my shirt. There is poop on it. Gross! Please."

She grabbed the scissors and made a jagged cut two inches above the poop in a big circle to be sure she made it completely around the entire sleeve, and then flung it in the bucket. That shirt could have cost me $100.00 and I would have done just the same. It was not fair, nor was it over because I had to go back in and face the music. It's like going under water, holding your breath and getting it done. I did it. We finished up, and it was over. It was most certainly a group effort.

Now, I reeked, or so I thought. Regardless, I was not going to walk into my house on Thanksgiving Day smelling like shit. The smell had engulfed my nose hairs, and I was stuck with it. I pulled my long hair towards my nose and turned my head with such disgust. Shit shampoo is what it smelled like. "Can I get new scrubs," I was bellowing out to anyone who would listen to me. Thank god for the shirt underneath, cuz I was ripping off my scrub top like it was on fire. Housekeeping, brought up the scrubs from the OR. They could not get there quick enough. Every second I waited felt like hours, and if you looked behind me it was like someone was cutting onions. There were teary eyes everywhere because of the odor. The scrubs arrived, and the only remnants of this day were the cut up green thermal shirt left in the staff bathroom.

Ganja

It was Saturday morning and I was listening to report on the very old fashioned tape recorder. I was drowsy as usual, when I quickly snapped out of lala land as report began on room 9. The nurse who was giving report is awesome. She gives a very informative report, and today she was exceptionally thorough. I wish you could hear her cute little voice when talking about this particular guy. We see some strange things here and we get to hear it all, but I tell ya...this story is Grade A product.

I'll call him Guy. Guy was a gentleman in his 60's, and he was a quadriplegic. I do not know all of the details that encompassed his hospitalization, and for this story, I didn't need to know it. The tape was rolling, and I heard, "So, he was caught smoking marijuana in his room." I immediately paused the tape. "Did anyone else hear that? Geez, he's smoking the ganja in there and making himself right at home." I couldn't believe what I was hearing. The dude was smoking a big fat bone in his room. I think he totally forgot where he was. Where the hell did he get this? He was a quad, so where was the joint hiding? The patient and the weed were the only two that knew the answer to that question. There would have been a day, years ago, when I would have said, "Oh, I don't believe this," and my jaw would be hitting the dirt on the floor, but with each passing day I am becoming more accustomed to the amazing idiosyncrasies of this business.

Guy has an un-stageable wound on his hip. What this means is that his wound was so large we were unable to put the wound in a particular category. There are four stages. Stage four is the deepest wound right down to the bone. Guy's wound was worse than that. Gaping would be a fine adjective to use in his case. Try to envision the wound in your mind. I myself did not see this, but many other people did when they had to care for him. He must have been hiding his stash in there. At some point during the evening shift he sparked up a bone. Naturally the smell was wafting up the hallway from one end to the other. The nurse went down there, low and behold, it was a joint! There was no denying that smell and the very fresh aroma of the marijuana pot plant. Even if you have never seen, touched or smoked the plant, there is no mistaking that smell. I am not being naive, nor can I give this guy the benefit of the doubt, but many if not everyone knows that pot is illegal when it is purchased on the street by a guy with no name and you refer to him by saying he is on the corner of Stupid Street and Moron Road. His desk was the corner curb. He doesn't have doctor's hours, and he

Brenda Wojick

works 24/7. Also, doctors do not pull out a Glock 9mm and shoot you for failing to make a copayment. For years and until this day, there is no smoking in a hospital. There is a little known gas called oxygen that could blow up when it comes in contact with a flammable substance. Oh, but this gets even more amusing. What should be done with the weed? Shall we smoke it? Shall we sell it? Wrong. We had to save it for him. We put it right with his belongings in a safe. When he left we had check that right off of his belongings sheet. Money, credit cards, glasses, dentures, pot....

Don't mind me

It was the day of a full moon and I was the charge nurse on for the day shift. I always hold my breath when I am in charge because it always becomes an interesting day. I was sitting up at the front of the desk going over the staffing schedule for the next shift, and I could feel someone hovering over me. He was casting a shadow over both myself and the desk. I glanced up and there was this old man, probably in his 80's, with scruffy facial hair that was almost all gray. He didn't have any teeth, but this didn't surprise me what-so-ever. Harry had this large indent on his face right where his oxygen tubing should have been. His Johnny was on the wrong way because he was trying to wear it as a bathrobe. He also had some blood stains on his Johnny. This look was not working for him. He could not breathe that well, and he used the desk to hold himself up. It appeared as if he was at the end of a bar in the local pub propped up on one elbow waiting for his drink to be served. I was the first to say something. "Well, hello." "Hey," he wheezed back.

I looked up from the computer I was on. "What can I do for ya my friend?" His reply was, "You can get me a couple of blondies and some busties." He sounded like he was highly intoxicated, slurring his words. I had an idea of what he meant, I am not so sure he knew, but I think he was trying to ask for boobies. Alrightly then. I was so glad I asked. He was making some pretty damn shallow panting sounds. "Let's go take a stroll down the hall and back to your room. With a very sadistic hollow, almost perverted chuckle, he said, "Close the door behind ya baby." I ignored the comment. "Let's get your oxygen back on and you have to get back into bed." As soon as the words left my mouth I knew the "bed" comment was going to set Smokey the Bandit up for his next line. "Why don't you come with me?" Ah, that would be another NO.

"Here we go, put your feet onto the bed. Up, up, up. Com'on. Here we go. Lean back onto the pillow." I set the bed alarm and I went back to finish my paperwork.

I was on the computer when Jen came up to me and said, "I smell something." I got up and went towards Harry's room and I could smell it. That would be cigarette smoke.

Knock, knock, knock

Knocking on a patient's door is done out of respect for their privacy. I knock, I go in. It's that simple. Well, not entirely. It most definitely has to do with who the individual is. Catherine came to get me down the hall to relay a message from Diane, the permanent tenant on our floor. The statement was made that I knocked on her door, but then I barged right in. I disagreed. I hardly thought that opening the door after knocking is barging in. Barging in would be your little brother snapping the door open when you are getting dressed, or when you are ready to squat over the toilet at your favorite restaurant, and for some reason you forgot to lock the door. The door is flung open and now you are face to face with a total stranger like a deer in the headlights. Now that's barging in.

You see, Diane was a control freak. She would even like to tell you how to enter and exit her room, how to knock, how to close the door.... not happenin'. The mistake was made on the day she was admitted – that was the actual mistake. This may sound cruel, and it is not meant

Brenda Wojick

to be. She was a paraplegic, and she did have a very sad past history, but nevertheless, it did not give her the right to walk all over the staff here and treat us like her personal assistants. The last time I looked, my paycheck did not reflect private duty nursing. After all, I am still human, people, although it may not always sound it in this book. I can empathize, but I will never be able to walk in her shoes.

The patient's room down the end of the hallway had now become "her room." Keep in mind that she was not paying rent on this room, but somehow she had managed to take over the four walls as if she were paying rent. She truly believed this was her own casa, so the only thing that needed to be done here was to have her sign a lease.

Knock, knock ..I waited patiently. "Who is it," I heard from behind the door in a muffled voice. There can only be a handful of different people that are knocking on the door. It could be a nurse, a doctor, nurse's aide, or food service personnel.

"It's Brenda," I said through clenched teeth. I thought I almost broke my front tooth I was gritting so tightly.

"Who?" Oh for the love of god, now she's busting my chops. I opened the door at this point. She could control some things, but not everything. She was downright rude. She was just not a nice person. I didn't put her in that bed, therefore I did not deserve to be shit upon the way she did to me all that day. Don't hate the playa girl, hate the game.

Can You Squeeze My Banana?

It was a Saturday and I had five patients to take care of, all busy little bees, and I also had to leave the floor to take part in a "disaster drill" that the hospital arranged. I believe it is a good thing to have training if ever an emergency situation were to arise. I looked at the clock. It was 10 am, and I still had a long time to go until it is the end of the day. Five and a half hours to be exact. So I was asked to be the designated person to go down to the "disaster drill". I figured, what the heck. It was better than dealing with the woman down the hallway. When I got downstairs to the emergency room I was a little uncomfortable seeing coworkers sporting their bathing suits. I am not quite sure what scenario the leaders of the drill depicted for a "disaster", but when these individuals were coming into the ER, they had supposedly been decontaminated somewhere along the line by a hose, thus being wrangled through the door like cattle, soaking wet and wearing their best swimsuit attire. I was supposed to be a nurse assisting in the plan gathering pertinent information thus stabilizing the patient that lay in front of me. It was very difficult to do such a thing and focus when I am checking out the 2009 designer line of swimwear. There was some staff that I recognized, but I could not remember their names for the life of me, and I do believe this was a positive thing. Looking past the modeling show, I realized that they were employees of the hospital. Suddenly one of the young girls that was in her 20's threw herself on the floor, apparently enthralled in her role as a victim in a hazardous waste drill. She dropped like a heavy

Brenda Wojick

sack of potatoes. I wouldn't drop my trash on the floor at any hospital, not just the hospital that I work in. Yes they are cleaned and sanitized the best that they can be, but just the thought of what was on the floor previous to this was quite disturbing to me. Examples of the possibilities would be: dirt, crap, dirty feet, soiled linen, boogies, blood…I'm sure you get the point. I don't even want to keep my clogs on the floor, but something has to come between my feet and the floor.

In another bed there was a young man getting into his role as well. He was yelling and apparently being the belligerent drunk. He too was once an employee of the hospital. I can say that everyone participating in this drill was going along with him until the transfer from the stretcher to the bed. This was when he let out a frightening shriek to the point where I almost shit my Victoria's Secret underwear. God did he scare me and everyone else. His appearance was as if he was having a gran mal seizure. What the hell man…He flopped onto the floor. Another one on the floor. What were these people thinking? Why the magnetic attraction to such a disturbing surface? Gross. I thought it was just about time to go back to my assignment upstairs, and that's exactly what I had to do.

The floor was exactly as I had left it. Calls bells were ringing, the clock on the wall was standing still, phones were ringing and the doctors were conversing, but it was still my comfort zone. It is still what I do.

Can You Squeeze My Banana?

It was Saturday, and I hate working the weekends, but I am not alone. Most nurses hate working weekends as well. I am not sure why. It is like any day of the week, but the difference with working a Saturday or Sunday is that no matter how chaotic my day may be, it is still a less stimulating day than midweek; most of the time. Managers, for the most part do not work weekends. Social work and case management are in hiding, the MD's are dressed down, and there seem to be fewer family members who come to visit, believe it or not. Some days it is almost eerie. Even the main hallways, for example, like the one down to the cafeteria are a lot quieter. It is almost like a chapter from Stephen King's book *The Langoliers* where everyone but 7 people disappear as they pass through the Aurora Borealis.

Moving right along, I had to go see my other patients. Next to Diane's room, apartment if you will, was a 6 foot tall 300 pound dude that I am taking care of who was curled up in his bed. Should he ring, he will get what he needs because he is scary looking. He was very intimidating. His hand appeared bigger than my whole damn face. He would be able to give me a scuff and a smack down at a moment's notice. His diagnosis was pneumonia, but his incentive and goal was to take all the Dilaudid he could. If you haven't already realized by reading this book, there are many people out there who absolutely love receiving Dilaudid. The numbers are astonishing and we have to deal with them all.

Brenda Wojick

Mike just had back surgery so I couldn't imagine the pain, but we were managing his pneumonia and his surgery was a couple of months back. He talked like the Godfather for all of you who know the great Marlon Brando. It was like he had a bag of cotton stuck in his jowls. He told me I was lazy and late when it came to bringing him his Dilaudid. I also had to worry about my other chickenella in the room next to him who apparently collected STD's for a living. It was a shame because she was a detoxing heroin injecting female who actually at one time had a decent life until she fell off the wagon. She was sweet to me unlike a "usual" detoxer. To support her drug habit she now owns herpes which you carry with you like luggage at all times. It is yours to keep forever and ever. She also has Chlamydia, a touch of gonorrhea and a sprinkle of trichinosis which doesn't sound really that bad.

Now that you all have vagina on the mind, I want to go back to Diane and collect the rent. She was ringing so now would be a good time, plus I had to give her Monistat. Who the hell in their right mind rings their bell so that they can receive their vag cream for their yeast infection? She does. I took a deep breath, twisted my head to the right and then to the left. I made a swinging motion as if I were practicing Tai Chi. I knocked, and you know I wouldn't forget after she put me in my place. After I was invited into her home she informed me that it was Monistat time. Now don't get this moment confused with Miller time. I was making hand motions as if I were actually excited to perform such a task. *O goody, pick me, pick me*!

"My Monistat is on the counter. You can do it now," she huffed at me. I couldn't wait. It was at the top of my list of to do's, breakfast, coffee, apply vag cream to Diane. In a tone that was calm and not abrasive, I said, "sure." Here it comes people, the million dollar question that left her mouth. "Do you know where you put the Monistat?" Any American who has ever watched TV and watched commercials on TV knows where the heck to put Monistat. You do not have to be a doctor to know this. My own kids can tell me. She just liked to be insulting any time she could. So I bit my tongue because I wanted to say to her, "I paste your mouth shut with it, right?" Instead I said, "of course I do."

"Well then, you know it goes into my vagina?" No one likes to say that word. It's a dirty word and it might even be forbidden in some parts of the world. She smirked as she said it. She has one eyebrow raised. It was after I caught the smirk that I noticed the two lop sided pony tails that stuck out of her head. How did I ever miss this? One was placed more at the top side of her head and the other at the bottom side. If you are 54 years old, you should not be wearing pig tails anyway, and if you do, someone should have the right to tell you how ridiculous you look. "What are you doing over there," she snapped. I couldn't even respond. I did not want to be rude.

Brenda Wojick

"You are going to need help putting that in." she said. Gosh, how big was her vagina that I needed help applying this? How many reinforcements do I need for this?

"I can do this, thank you though for your concern," I replied. I went to apply the cream, I will spare you the details, and she asked, "how does my vagina look down there?" There's that friggin' word again. I knew what I was looking at. She didn't need to state the obvious, besides, what it god's name is she asking me this for? It looked like a vajay jay. Was it supposed to look more glamorous than others? "Ah, it looks good," I said. I raised my eyebrows in hopes that I answered the question correctly.

"Did you wipe my vagina?"

"Ya, I wiped your vagina." Now she had me saying it.

"You can go now," she said as she waved me off and dismissed me in a flash. Now I knew what it was like to be dissed after a one night stand. I felt so violated.

My guy next door was mad at me, as he told one of the tech's that answered his call bell. I was late with his pain meds. So when I went in to give him the Dilaudid, he was fast asleep. Huh? He wanted to leave against medical advice, I said, go for it, but he didn't. He stayed. The doctor convinced him to stay. Meanwhile, we had a lady down the hallway, and I answered her bell when it was ringing. I ended up putting her on the bedpan. She was scary. She was a black female, and her eyes

220

Can You Squeeze My Banana?

were wide open. It didn't appear as if she could even blink, and when she talked to me it sounded as if she was speaking in tongues to me. I really couldn't understand what she was saying. When I walked by her room later in the day I could have sworn that she had a voodoo doll of me, and as I started to get a headache that day, I really thought she was the one putting the pins into the top of my head.

By the time I thought I could do some paperwork, Diane had rung again. It was time for her pain medication and potassium supplement. I walked down there with both. I put the liquid potassium on the table, and I put down the water next to it for her to take. "What is this?" she wanted to know. "Well, it is your potassium with some water."

"I take it with half a glass of cranberry juice with the potassium mixed in it. If it is more than a half a cup, I will have you start over again." I apparently was not her usual bartender because I had gotten her drink wrong. Finally after two tries, I got the mixture right. I was able to leave her room yet again. I had so much more to do for her, but guess what, it would have to be tomorrow when I came back because folks, my day was done for today.

Give Her a Parking Ticket

I walked down the hall and there she was, Mary parked in the hallway in her bed, IV pole long and lean by her side. She was flagging down anybody in the hallway that she could possibly flag down. She looked rather bizarre. I am used to seeing patients in chairs out in the hallway, but never in the entire bed. She in the huge bed she was completely out of place. Underneath all the white linens was a little old lady is peering over her marshmallow like blanket waiting for the world to wake up, come alive and tend to her every need. Her 98 year old bottom lip was hanging far enough south to be almost brushing against the tiny fibers of the blanket. That was one very old lip. She appeared to be approximately 4 feet and a couple of inches tall. She was probably at least 5 feet tall back in the day until osteoporosis set in and shrunk her back in time. We had no choice but to sandwich her in between the bed because of her frequent falls at her nursing home. The head of the bed goes up and the foot of the bed folds up as well. Mary is now the

222

cream filling of an Oreo cookie. She was not moving anywhere, and just to make sure, the bed alarm was on as well.

The reason for her hospitalization was the nasty fall she took at the nursing facility that she called home, that actually wedged her between her tub and her sink when she went to wash her hands after peeing. After she was pulled from the wreckage and freed from her nightmarish ordeal, she arrived on my floor with a fractured pelvis and swollen, ecchymotic left shoulder that was heavily guarded and in a locked position by a blue sling. She was not moving that arm for all the tea in China.

She did not come to the hospital with her hearing aids in. They were left at the nursing home, so communicating was a huge challenge. It was a shouting match with myself because either way she was not hearing me. She was looking at one of the techs while I was speaking to her. It was if I was throwing my voice in a poor act of ventriloquism. She didn't want to be bothered at all, and she made this wish of hers known loud and clear. She also made everything else she had to say known loud and clear. Her favorite toy of all became her voice, and she loved to throw it around. When she needed to get our attention she yelled and yelled, and then yelled some more. We even opened up the blinds in her room so that she would be able to see all the little busy bodies in the hallway so that she did not feel alone. It almost worked, but not quite.

Brenda Wojick

Something caught my eye as I walked from her room. It was a little old guy, probably in his 80's, all hunched forward. His motion was subtle enough that he almost slipped by my sight. I could see him shuffling to his right side leaving one room and going into another. This action was what really snagged my attention, or maybe it was his half nakedness as his scrawny body was clad only in a baby blue depends. He was holding up each side of his diaper by tugging at the top of plastic that makes up temporary toileting device. It was then that I realized what was going on when I saw the nurse's aides running down the hall and heard a bed alarm was going off. He was escaping! Not only was he escaping, he was seeking refuge in another patient's room. The particular patient that was occupying the room next to him happened to be much younger than he, probably in her 40's. The girls had to get him quickly. I had to get him quickly. We came and conquered just in the nick of time. At least by the time I made it to the room where he was hiding in, he was in the middle of the room, squatting down, attempting to remove his plastic drape that hung off of his 80 lb body frame. He was looking to go to the bathroom right there in the middle of the floor. "Oh my god, someone get him," is all I heard. Two of the girls charged him to stop a possibly messy situation. We had success. He was captured and taken into custody to be returned to his own room. The situation could have been a lot more gruesome had the perpetrator not been apprehended in time.

Christopher Columbus Day

"After two days in hospital I took a turn for the nurse"

W.C. Fields

Out there in the world there are some dirty boys. Most girls at one time in their life they have been attracted to a "dirty boy" or "bad boy" if you will. In fact, I have my very own "dirty boy" at home -my husband. (wink, wink) There is just something about them, that no matter how fresh they are, that you find yourself totally and utterly attracted to them. The nice boy always got the bad rap of being too nice. That wasn't fun. There is no challenge in someone who wants to do everything for you. That would be too easy. Most girls want a challenge in a relationship. Then there are these "dirty boys" that come to 3 and they really are D-I-R-T-Y, as in gross, odiferous and just plain dank. I don't think their mamas ever taught them good hygiene. Either that or they just didn't listen to her, and either way these boys put the capital S in skank.

Brenda Wojick

On Christopher Columbus day, that day that celebrates the landing of Christopher Columbus in America, I drove to the hospital in my minivan and discovered a very long day ahead of me, and one big "dirty boy" and that is not the "dirty bad boy". I am talking just plain nasty. My name will never go down in history as it did with Christopher Columbus although it should just for caring for this fella for 12 hours. I said a prayer, looked up at the sky, kissed the tips of my fingers as if looking for a favor, and said, "thank you." Then I started my day.

I went in to his room with somewhat of a positive attitude, and a smile on my face, and then my eyes met his. I actually winced in pain and shut my eyes. He was indeed the bête noire a.k.a the evil one, and it was at this time I realized I would much rather be taking care of the guy in room 10 who just took a shit that was so big that it had to be cut up before it could go down the toilet, and it was not me who had to disassemble it. There was going to be some gigantic problems that lay ahead because I was going to be the adversary that came between him and his Dilaudid. Right from the start he just gave me the damn willies.

He was a 34 year old chap with tan colored skin, and tattoos on his arms that didn't appear to have any rhyme or reason. He was most definitely a supersized gentleman who was short in stature when he stood up. He resembled humpty dumpty with an egg-like shape to him, and when he did get up, which was a rare event, he could very well topple over. There was most definitely a trifling aroma in the air which one could assume came from the many fat folds that his body contained. This could be a very fatiguing situation for even the most compassionate nurse in the field. There were some sparse follicles of hair that lay on the back of his dome, and for what he lacked in his head, he made up for in back hair. It appeared that he had a built in poncho, one big black poncho. When I put my stethoscope on his back to listen to his lung sounds, I lost my stethoscope. It never made it back out to me. It was lost in the poncho forever.

Now I know you've heard this one before, but his call light was on every two hours before he was due to his pain medication which happened to be Dilaudid. Patients love this stuff. I wouldn't know the feeling because I have never needed the stuff, thank god for that. As a nurse you know the people who are sick and truly in pain and really need that drug, and on the other end of the spectrum I can also point out the playa's of the healthcare system, and 99.9% of the time, I am correct. They are just looking for a high. Pain is a subjective symptom, and it is their word against mine. They win!!! Had this squirt been in that much pain, he would not have been begging me for a tuna fish sandwich.

Eduardo came through the Emergency department with upper left abdominal pain. You pancreas is in that quadrant of your abdomen. When you have pancreatitis you can be in a great deal of discomfort and torment and a tuna fish sandwich would not be on your to do list for the day. Curling up in a great big ball would be. This fine young chap refused to let the nursing staff give him Dilaudid subcutaneously. When you get it this way, the effects of the medication stay in your system and last longer. When you receive it intravenously, it penetrates your system in a much quicker way, but it does not stay in your system that long. This way creates a magical wonderland for the mind and body. His call bell would go off, and either myself or someone else would answer it and see what he needed.

"Eduardo, what can I do for ya," I would say, knowing exactly what he needed.

"Can I get some pain medication?" was always his answer.

"Sure," I would say, "but you know you have 25 minutes left before I can give it to you." He can have this every two hours. Not a tremendous amount of time to wait. "Can't you just give it to me now? No one will know."

"Sorry buddy. Call me crazy, but I am a nurse that plays by the rules."

"C'mon, you would be." Ya, that was his response. I attempted to wait out the 25 minutes, but he rang the call bell at least two more times. "Can I get my pain stuff?" "Okay, ringing the bell does not allow me to get your pain medication any quicker."

Can You Squeeze My Banana?

"Oh, did I ring that bell? I must have done that by accident." Lame response. I wasn't born yesterday. I bring in the pain med after a full 25 minutes, and now I had to sit in the room with this guy for 15 minutes while I pushed the Dilaudid and took his vital signs, which is a protocol that we must follow for the administration of this particular drug. Every two hours I had to do this and every two hours it was the longest 15 minutes of my existence. Same questions over and over, and same complaints were being made.

"Hey, can you get me some cranberry juice?" he whispered. "I can't. Now you know that when you are here for pancreatitis having had this situation before, you know that you cannot receive anything to eat or drink."

"Oh, yeah, you're the nurse that plays by the book. The other nurses snuck me in some last night. I told them I wouldn't tell anybody."

My response to that was, "Then why are you telling me? You are essentially "ratting out" a fellow nurse of mine. I also know for a fact that that particular nurse on the night shift told me you wanted some juice but she wouldn't bring it in either. So you can just try every shift if you want, but everyone's answer will ultimately be the same, NO."

"I can't believe you nurses talk to each other that much, even about little things like juice," he said.

Brenda Wojick

"Having something as little as juice can really bother you, and yes, we talk about everything when we give each other report. That would be called our job."

"Figures, nurses who stick together," was his response.

I administered the medication through his IV each time, and each time his head fell back, and his eyes rolled with his head, and he automatically let out a snort which was his body's attempt at a snore. He was then down for the count. He would just up and say the pain medication was working, and when I would describe what he looked like after the administration of the magical candy, he said I was lying, that he didn't do that. As much as I wanted the challenge of arguing, I didn't. He would be fast asleep and the second he would see me poke into his room he would clutch his stomach and moan in pain. He just kept wanting more and more. Nothing was going to be good enough for him. This went on for my entire shift, which was 7am to 7pm. Even the holiday pay wasn't making me smile at this point. Now he wanted a cigarette. Again, if you are in that much pain, you really would not want a cigarette. He was threatening to go out. I told him I could call security. You see, if a patient is on that much Dilaudid to the point where his eyes roll into the back of their head, I can't let them out to smoke a cigarette that is going to make them even more lightheaded. He said he would sign out AMA – against medical advice. I said, "Let me get the paper for you to sign that we are not liable in any way." This could be my early Christmas present. Just as I was getting the paperwork the doctor made it to the floor, and I explained everything to him about this knucklehead. The MD decided to try to appease him just once and let him go out for a cigarette, hoping this would calm him down for the rest of the evening. Now he was begging for the cigarette. I don't smoke. I am not taking him out. You see the stipulation was that someone had to bring him outside because his cigarettes were in his car in the garage. No female employee was to escort him out to the car. Excellent decision. So we needed someone willing to take him out with security to escort the big baby to his car. I got a hold of the nursing supervisor to take him out and meet with security. It was going to take time for her to get here because his smoking a butt was no one's priority at this time. He bitched and moaned for two hours. Again, I tried to sell him on signing the AMA papers. No such luck. I had another two hours of him leaning on the call bell, then another dose of Dilaudid, another bitch, another moan. I needed a glass of wine.

Finally, he could be taken down for a cig. Whew…ten minutes where I can get some work done. When the supervisor came back up she informed me that after all his whining, ranting and raving he got to his car, and he didn't have any cigarettes of his own. After all that. He said to the supervisor, "I thought you were going to get me a cigarette from someone." Now he wants us to supply his habit. Was he for real? That was the last straw.….

Brenda Wojick

What was really the last straw was the fact that his Dilaudid got changed to subcutaneous on the night shift. If you are going out to smoke, begging for tuna, and crying for cranberry juice, you can have your medication changed. Yes!!!! This will do the trick, and it did. He was given the benefit of the doubt, but most nurses know the kind. As soon as he realized that his medication was changed to subcutaneously, he was outta there. Bon voyage, brother. He left the hospital that night. He would eventually end up at another hospital's emergency room begging for the same kind of candy. Whateva! I had another big boy to contend to.

This was another gentleman who was 39 years old, and he was admitted for left axilla cellulitis. In laymen's terms, he had a red, swollen area under his armpit. It was not treated, and it became infected. When infection on the skin grows it becomes cellulitis, and a lot of times has to be lanced or drained. Yummy. Then the infection leaks out and it starts to heal. Some people are "dirty birds". That is a nice way of saying they don't wash themselves. Gathering from the enormous head sized whole in the heel of his tube sock, hygiene was not this guy's number one priority. What was it with these young men this week? All he had to do as part of his treatment was take a shower two times a day to put his left arm pit under the water because the surgeon had opened it up and drained it. The nurses were responsible for dressing the site and making sure he took the shower.

Can You Squeeze My Banana?

We got to chatting as I'm in there assessing this gentleman. He decides to offer the information, "I used to be engaged back in 1995. It didn't work. I need to get back onto the dating scene. It's been a little while." Whew….ya think? 14 years is more than a little while. That's an eternity for some. God, what was his purpose for telling me this because I was so uncomfortable. It might have something to do with the cellulitis or the big hole in his sock, who the hell knows. Oh, I got it…it is probably the fact that he is 39 and he still lives with his mother and father. He may want to branch out and get a place of his own. It's hard to date when you are sitting in between your parents. I was nice and told him not to get discouraged.

"All right, you need to take your shower John."

"I can't. Not until my mother brings in my underwear." How 'bout some damn socks, dude is what I was thinking.

"Well, why don't you take a shower, put on a Johnny and then when your mother gets here you can put on your crisp, fresh new undies. How's that sound for a plan?"

Reluctantly, he got up and went into the shower. Less than 5 minutes went by and he was back in his room waiting for me to dress his wound. His hair was perfectly dry, and the tape marks on the other arm that didn't need to get wet weren't wet. It was as dry as a bone. Same holey sock, same icky undies. I dressed his wound and went on my way.

233

Brenda Wojick

Then he called and I went in to check on him. He proceeded to tell me, "Brenda, I think I did something in my pants." Now, remember he is a 39 year old fully ambulatory, alert and oriented young man and now he has just announced to me that he shit his underwear. Oh, my god, I was mortified. Even if I did shit my pants and I was him, I would never call in the young nurse taking care of me and announce it to her. I would be burying my fruit of the loom so far in the bucket as possible. "Ah hah, okay." He got up and turned around to show me what he did like a proud little two year old. "Ah, ya. I think ya did. You might want to check on that situation there John." What else can I say? He turned and his gigantic underwear had the biggest streak from the bottom up to his back bone. He was proud and he was showing it. There was no sense of remorse, not one iota of embarrassment. I think I know why he's single ladies. I walked out. There was nothing I can do for him. I wasn't wipin' his 39 year old ass. He was quite capable of doing that himself.

At some point during the day, the surgeon came in and had to lance that area one more time. It had some more pus to drain. So the surgeon left the area open and wanted him to shower again. Apparently John wasn't up for shower number two. He wanted the area dressed. He was mad that I didn't run in there to take care of it, forgetting that I had other patients to tend to. He decided to take it out on one of the nursing assistants. She went in there to tell him I would be in there shortly, and that was not good enough. He threw the pillow against the wall like a big baby, and started yelling, "Fuck you, or fuck this place." Hurling a big white fluffy pillow at the wall. Ooohhh, tough boy. Flinging pillows at people. Be careful not to crap yo'self again. He also told her that I do not spend enough time in there talking to him. Boo hoo! I was doing something else at this point, and I must say, I practically jogged down there to see what his problem was. Now, I am not in the business of bullying my patients, but they should not bully the staff, if you call throwing a pillow bullying.

"John, I have other people to see, you need another shower as part of your treatment, and then I will redress your wound. You do not have to yell obscenities at staff members or throw pillows at anyone, thank you very much."

"I'm sorry, I'm sorry," he said. "I just want to be taken care of."

I was not his mother, I wasn't going to give him clean socks or change his shitty diapers. I was his nurse and I would do what I had to do, but clearly not that. I practically pulled him out of bed for the shower. My friend Karen said all she could see was his body, and then me hiding behind it because he was so large. His head was hung low, and it was like walking the Green Mile, slow and treacherous. Who knew a shower could be so bad. Most patients would kill for one. Not him. He came back out dry as a bone, with hair that was not wet. I went in and covered up his incision. My goodness did he whimper. He

Brenda Wojick

was biting down on the pillow that he secured over his face. One might have thought I was torturing him if they passed by the room. The only person being tortured was me. It was time for me to leave.

Puff the Magic Dragon

"I'm here to take Evelyn for an x-ray, and she is not in her room. Do you know who has her," the transport man asked me. The transport team is what we call the department of people who help us tremendously. They not only help us, they help the whole hospital, and we rely on them for getting our patients in and out of the hospital and to and from tests. They wear green button down shirts to identify themselves, and to be quite honest they are the only individuals who know how to drive those damn stretchers from one place to another. Those beds have a mind of their own, and if you are not careful, you can get into a mighty big accident.

I once attempted to bring a patient back from x-ray because transport was backed up and it took me practically 20 minutes to get the person just to the elevator which was no more than 100 feet away. Now, getting her into the actual elevator was a big ordeal. The stretchers come with levers on the bottom of the bed to lock, to go straight, or to steer. I figured this out the hard way when I was trying to turn into the elevator

Brenda Wojick

and the bed wouldn't budge. I was so embarrassed. I must have looked like a complete shmuck. I was trying so hard not to bounce the fragile little soul off of the elevator doors. I finally made it to my floor. It was a major milestone, and I would not go back and do that ever again. I do my job because I can do it and I don't expect any other department to know how to, and this holds very true for the transport department. I will leave their job up to them.

So, I had to go see where Evelyn went. I remember her telling me she didn't smoke, so that means that she was out having a cigarette. It was not hard at all to see the pack of Marlboro's that she had next to her that morning when I introduced myself. I went in to assess her wheezy lung sounds, and I saw the bright red and white square box next to her along with her yellow fingernails which is very indicative of someone who smokes a lot. At one point that morning she told me that she was going out to get some "air." The only people who want to get air around this joint are the people who smoke. They will find any way to escape through the double doors that are at the far end of the corridor. Evelyn has been a patient on our floor for about a week, and since she's been here she is in a wheelchair at all times, and she is off the floor more than she is on the floor. We have not been able to keep her in her room long enough to talk to her.

"Let's go," I said to the transport kid. He was a kid, and by kid I mean he was not my age. I motioned to him with my head and he

238

Can You Squeeze My Banana?

followed. He probably took one look at my face and realized I was pissed, so he just followed. I didn't mean anything towards him. This patient had just got my panties in a bunch. We walked all the way down the hallway past the cafeteria and out the side doors. There she was in her wheelchair with her kids at her side, and she took one look at me and realized she needed to flick that cigarette and quick. Although, come to think of it, she probably didn't care. She just didn't want to have to hear my lecture. I pointed to her.

"There's the patient," I said to the transport kid. "Evelyn, this young man is here to take you down to your chest x-ray which you will go down now because we can't keep chasing you down to take care of you. So he is going to take you now. You are already in the wheelchair, it makes it that much easier." I motioned again to the transport kid, "You can take her now, please. Thanks." He nodded, "You're welcome."

"I'm back," I announced when I came back on the floor. I was telling one of the other nurses, "For crying out loud, Evelyn was outside smoking again. I had to go track her down to get her to go for an x-ray."

"Brenda, x-ray on line one for you," the secretary called out. I picked up the phone. "It's Brenda, how can I help you?"

"We have your patient down here for chest x-ray and she is breathing pretty hard saying she's having some shortness of breath."

239

Brenda Wojick

"Well, she should have shortness of breath because I just found her outside with a butt in her mouth. I practically had to pry it out so she would down and see you guys."

The girl on the other line let out a chuckle, "Well, that would explain why she sounds huffy and puffy." We both had to laugh because this situation was completely ridiculous. People are out there fighting to be seen by doctors, and this lady was admitted for help and she completely disobeys every rule. She should not be here. "Ah, send her back when you are done with her. I'm sure she will make a pit stop on the way back up and smoke another ciggie butt." There was more laughter. Believe it or not, stories like this are a dime a dozen. You can't imagine how many people are noncompliant. The moment transport wheeled her back up to her room, her kids were taking her back down for a cigarette. We should have the cigarette police out there because we could use them right now. Finally Evelyn now came back to her room, and I know this because her call bell was going off. When I went down there to see what she wanted, she asked for a breathing treatment. Why in the world would she ever need a nebulizer treatment? Was she kidding me? Her lungs are tight and she needs to open them up to let some more shit in. She told me that she had blood clots in her legs, but refused to take the medication that prevents them. She was coughing up a lung, making some gawd awful noise as she was doing it, but yet refusing to

240

Can You Squeeze My Banana?

take Mucinex, the medicine that helps bring up the junk in her lungs. She needed to go!

I had one day off and when I came back she had left the hospital against medical advice, which was fine. She was not following what she should have been doing. Guess what? Sunday night before the end of my shift we had a new admission, and here came Evelyn riding up on a stretcher arguing with everyone. She didn't want to be here. Well, we all voted that she not come here either. She didn't want anyone to treat her -not the doctors or nurses. She had young kids with her and I couldn't imagine letting my kids see me like this. I never knew what happened with her because it was time for me to leave. This case was creating so much drama, and this is exactly what Evelyn wanted, drama!

Food for Thought

"The most powerful force in the universe is gossip"

Dave Barry

Do you know what stinks?? Giving a patient an intramuscular injection and having it hit bone. There is no worse feeling in the world than jabbing it in and having it recoil back at ya...

Do you know what stinks worse than that? Doing that same thing again!

Why would anyone listen to an overweight dietician?

Would you ever trust a respiratory therapist who smokes?

Going into a patient's room and finding their family member making themselves at home lying in their bed.

Patient peeing in his wash basin.

Pet Peeves

1. I was once listening for a patient's heart rate and rhythm. Seems easy enough, we all know where our heart is; only this time I can't find it. I feel stupid. She's alive and talking, breathing and blinking. Where the hell is her heart? I think that she is getting a kick out of this. She actually had an anomaly and her heart was on the right side of her chest wall. Don't you just hate that?

2. Irritating…receiving a report that a patient has bilateral positive pedal pulses only the patient has no right leg.

3. When a male patient wants to show me his penile implant.

4. A female patient that is talking to you and her false teeth fall out onto her lap.

5. Hearing a patient yelling for help at the end of the hallway that she can't see, and when I run down there, she has her wig pulled down over her eyes. (that's actually funny)

6. Answering someone's call bell because that person rang it himself. When I approach the room to see of how I can

be of assistance I am asked, "What button do I use to call you?" Dah!!!

7. A patient who answers their TV clicker and tried to change the phone.

8. A family member approached me to see if her husband will be discharged by the weekend. She was having a lot of company and wanted to know. I told her that I didn't know, it would clearly be up to his physician. She asked me, "Can he stay here this weekend?"

9. There is nothing worse than getting stool specimens. (this could also be a pet peeve)

10. Peeling a bandage from a wound and skin and the scab come off with it. Ewwww!

11. Patient's who leave AMA (against medical advice) but want you to call them a cab, wheel them to the front door, order their lunch before they go.

12. There is nothing worse than rolling a patient to clean him and he lets out an enormous shart. (shit and a fart) Gross!

13. I hate when a family member calls the floor and says, "Hi, I am Lisa Deat, and I'm calling about my mother. How is she doing?" Now don't you think a name would help.

14. When one of the nursing assistants went into this particular female patient's room, which by the way is in her 80's, to

check on her, she went in and asked, "What are you doing"? Very nonchalantly because it is an everyday questions that we ask. The patient's response was, "I'm masturbating, what the hell do you think I'm doing."

15. One of the nursing assistants was talking to the same patient when the female patient decided to just simply state to her "You know, oral sex never did anything for me. I can't see dragging my tongue up and down."

16. One cute little elderly lady asked right before discharge, "Can you ask the doctor for a prescription for ice cubes?"

17. One person was on the floor for withdrawing from opiates. When asked why he came in for treatment was, "My dealer had a heart attack and died."

18. An elderly patient had terminal cancer and did not have much longer to live. The family of the patient was refusing to make her a DNR (Do Not Resuscitate) but they asked if we could do "gentle chest compressions" if she coded. Apparently they do not know what CPR means. There's nothing gentle about it.

19. We had a patient that you thought was cute until you actually got to take care of her. She wasn't so cute then. She was walking in the hallway and then back to her room when she started to yell, "I'm scared, I'm scared." The nurse asked,

"Why are you scared?" The best response ever came out of her mouth, "I'm scared of the color of my pocketbook."

20. This little old lady, she was anything but cute, was assisted into the ladies room. She was very unsteady so myself and a coworker waited for her. This is what she had to say to us, "It's been so long since I had sex, I think I grew a new hymen." She's 79, I don't even want to think about it, and I sure as well don't want to know why she would remember what a hymen even was.

21. Patient's family asks if their father will need dialysis FOREVER. He's 98 years old. Forever might only be 10 more minutes.

22. During the initial assessment when the patient is admitted we ask a series of questions, one being "What helps you cope with stress?" His response was a classic, "My bartender."

23. I walked by a patient's room and she had a pair of the mesh panties on her head. That wasn't even the part that had the nurses turning their heads. It was when you took a closer look at that underwear that we noticed they had a poop streak on them.

24. I had this patient who was withdrawing from heroin, but she was rinsing out her mouth after her inhaler as the directions stated. Now she's compliant.

25. An elderly female was admitted unfortunately to detox. The next part was the strange part. She was detoxing from Listerine. Yes, Listerine. Her family found over 10 empty bottles of it around her house.

26. One of my patient's once said, "I don't like wearing a Johnny, it makes me look sick."

27. A female patient asked one of the doctors on the floor, "what is that?" He replied, "My shoe." She asked, "Can I go in it?"

28. "Good morning," I said to my patient. "How are you feeling?" "I don't feel." He said.

29. One of the nurse's assistants had asked a cute little old lady, "Are you having any pain?" Her response was, "No, honey, just a cookie."

30. I asked a confused patient, "Do you know where you are?" meaning which hospital are you in. Her response, "Yeah, I'm in a bed."

31. For two days we saw this man coming down the hallway on the even side with a little duffle bag in his hand, dark hair, disheveled looking. He would always leave clean, shaven, hair slicked back. We finally realized that this guy was homeless, and he was coming to our floor to use the shower. Can you imagine?

Brenda Wojick

(1) Careers.stateuniversity.com

(2) http://malaysia.answers.yahoo.com/question/
     index?qid=20080226040117AA61yfv

(3) http://mw1.merriam-webster.com/dictionary/servant

LaVergne, TN USA
08 September 2010
196352LV00001B/154/P